A
Guide to Better Punctuation

Second Edition

D0709071

Angela Burt

Stanley Thornes (Publishers) Ltd

First published in 1983 (ISBN 0–85950–105–1)
Second edition published in 1991 by:
Stanley Thornes (Publishers) Ltd
Ellenborough House
Wellington Street
CHELTENHAM GL50 1YD
UK

Reprinted 1993

British Library Cataloguing in Publication Data
Burt, Angela
    A Guide to better punctuation. – 2nd ed.
    I. Title
    421
    ISBN 0–7487–1122–8

Typeset by Tech-Set, Gateshead, Tyne & Wear.
Printed and bound in Great Britain at The Bath Press, Avon.

CONTENTS

ACKNOWLEDGEMENTS

The author and publishers are grateful to the following for permission to reproduce extracts and articles:

The Bodley Head, *The Private World of Georgette Heyer* by Jane Aitken Lodge; Brian Bell for his article 'Exhausting Round' from *The Times Educational Supplement*; Curtis Brown on behalf of the Estate of Sir Winston Churchill, *My Early Life* by Sir Winston Churchill; the *Daily Mirror* for 'Mrs T'; The Dramatic Publishing Company, 123 Sharp Hill Road, Wilton, Connecticut 06897, USA, for the play of *To Kill a Mockingbird* by Christopher Sergel; Eric Chisholm for his letter 'Metaphorical mix-up' from *The Times*; the *Express and Echo* for 'Smokers'; Grafton Books (HarperCollins Publishers) for 'i thank you god' from *The Complete Poems* by e. e. cummings; Hamish Hamilton Ltd, *Across the Barricades* by Joan Lingard; HMSO, *Proposals for the English Curriculum* (with the permission of the Controller of Her Majesty's Stationery Office); The Hogarth Press, *Cider With Rosie* by Laurie Lee; Hutchison Publishing Company, *With Great Pleasure* by Alec Reid; *The Independent* for 'Greenies who deserve 1001 Brownie points' by Diana Hinds, 'Question of degree', 'CFC substitutes "cause warming" ' by Nicholas Schoon, 'Conquered by the Classics'; John Rayment, President of the Essex Society for Family History, for 'Names in Fiction'; Jonathan Cape Ltd, *Look at Me* by Anita Brookner and *The Silver Sword* by Ian Serraillier; Optima Books, *Stress and Relaxation* by Jane Maddens; Peter Fraser and Dunlop Group Ltd, *Solitude* by Anthony Storr; Rachel Lindsay for 'The Congo' from *Poetry for Today* edited by George Mac Beth; reproduced by permission of Rogers, Coleridge and White Ltd, *In Custody* by Anita Desai, published by Penguin Books and by William Heinemann. Scripture quotations taken from the *Holy Bible, New International Version*. © 1973, 1978, 1984 by International Bible Society. Used by permission. Times Newspapers Ltd, 'Ship ahoy in back garden', 'Mixed-up mongrels make work for pet psychiatrists' by Hugh Thompson, 'Davy's lamp loses its spark', 'Battle of the bimbos' by Hugh Thompson; Veritas Publications, *First Steps in Counselling* by Ursula O'Farrell.

Every effort has been made to contact copyright holders and we apologise if any have been overlooked.

PREFACE

This new edition of *A Guide to Better Punctuation* has been prepared, at the invitation of my publisher, to meet the requirements of the National Curriculum at Key Stages 2, 3 and 4, while continuing to be of interest to sixth form and college students, and to the general public.

The text is now not only fuller but the presentation is livelier, thanks to Tim Archbold's cartoons. In addition, I have been permitted to use extracts from newspaper articles, published letters, handbooks and contemporary literature to illustrate the function of punctuation in context and to provide the basis for a generous number of practice exercises. In many of these exercises, I have encouraged analytical discussion and some have been structured for pair and group work.

I hope to show that there is nothing mysterious or arcane about the functions of the full stop, the comma, the capital letter, the apostrophe, the exclamation mark, the question mark, the colon, the semi-colon, inverted commas, the dash, the hyphen, the oblique and brackets. Each has a specific contribution to make to written expression, and that contribution can sometimes be a fascinating one.

The function of punctuation in writing is particularly well expressed in paragraph 3.9 of the Department of Education and Science's *English from 5 to 16*, 2nd edition, (HMSO, 1986):

> Punctuation needs more attention in English teaching than it sometimes receives. It is a systematic aspect of the written language and essential to meaning, for it performs two vital functions. One is the grammatical function of making clear the relationship between parts of sentences and of paragraphs. The other is the rhetorical function of indicating tone, attitude, feeling and emphasis. In speech, both these functions are carried out by such means as

pause, pitch, pace, intonation and volume, often accompanied by facial expression and gesture. In the written language, accurate punctuation is the necessary substitute for these resources.

I hope that all those who use this workbook will be enabled to punctuate their own written work with just such insight and confidence. I hope also that they will discover that they read the carefully written work of others with increased pleasure and understanding.

This workbook is intended for class use and for individual study. The practice exercises are designed to enable all students to score high marks if they apply the straightforward guidelines embodied in the text. There is a full explanation of each point, and exercises are set at each stage to reinforce the reader's understanding.

There is a logical progression from one unit to the next but I have made each unit as self-contained as possible so that students can be directed towards a particular unit if they are persistently making errors in the use of a particular punctuation mark. (Answers to the exercises are given at the back of the book for the benefit of those who are studying on their own.)

Angela Burt
Exmouth 1991

Chapter One

FULL STOPS, QUESTION MARKS, EXCLAMATION MARKS

Full stops, questions marks and exclamation marks have one important function in common; they all mark the ends of sentences whether those sentences are statements, questions or commands.

Such 'end stops' are vital to the understanding of a written text. Even a short passage becomes very confusing without these signals; the reader needs to know where one sentence ends and another begins if the passage is to be read with any fluency.

You can test this by trying to read aloud without hesitation and without preparation the short passage below.

Please send your reply to this query by return this Tuesday we have a Board Meeting and the matter will be discussed.

under 'Any Other Business', on Friday we'll be passing through Paris,too late to collect your reply personally but perhaps we could at least have dinner together.

Once you've sorted out where the sentence boundaries are, of course, the meaning becomes clear. A carefully punctuated text removes ambiguities and confusions. When the structure of each sentence is revealed, the reader's progress is made smooth.

Ensure that you are able to extend the courtesy of accurate punctuation to your readers.

Full stops

Each completed statement requires a **full stop** at the end.

The small news item below from *The Sunday Times* (note the date) will provide us with a two-paragraphed example of completed statements. Read the article carefully, noting where the full stops come. Make sure you can see the logical basis for punctuating the item as it has been punctuated.

Ship ahoy in back garden

A family from Selsey, near Chichester, were woken at 3.30 a.m. yesterday to find a 300-ton Danish coaster in the back garden of their beach-front home. Oliver Graham-Jones, 71, a vet, peered from his bedroom window and saw a hull with flashing lights looming a few feet away.

"The crew were a bit quiet about the whole thing and I think they were certainly embarrassed," he said. A crewman later said he thought he was in France. The unladen Platessa, en route from Falmouth to Hook of Holland, had gone through a gap in the sea wall. The ship was refloated on the afternoon tide.

© *The Sunday Times*, 1 April 1990

You can, of course, re-cast the whole item into *differently constructed* sentences. The first paragraph could quite easily become four sentences:

> A family from Selsey, near Chichester, were woken at 3.30 a.m. yesterday. They found a 300-ton Danish coaster in the back garden of their beach-front home. Oliver Graham-Jones, 71, a vet, peered from his bedroom window. He saw a hull with flashing lights looming a few feet away.

Moreover, you could break these four sentences down into many more smaller sentences. Stylistically it will make the item very boring but it will help to show that sentences are self-contained completed statements.

> Selsey is near Chichester. The Graham-Jones family lives in Selsey. They were woken yesterday at 3.30 a.m. Their home is a beach-front house. In their back garden they found a Danish coaster. It weighed 300 tons . . .

Given the same information, no two writers would express themselves in exactly the same way. As a writer, you can control the amount of information and detail you want to put into each sentence that you write. However, when each sentence is complete, remember to use an 'end stop' (a full stop, question mark or exclamation mark) as a guide to your reader.

A common error is to string together completed statements with commas instead of using full stops to separate them.

In Exercise 1, five full stops should be substituted for carelessly used commas.

Exercise 1

Replace five of the commas with full stops where they are needed.

1) I am hungry, is there anything to eat?

2) Although the house looked very dilapidated, it was a bargain at £30,000.

3) The cake should be cooked for three hours in a slow oven, don't be tempted to open the oven door before the cake is cooked.

4) The BBC wishes to apologise to Mrs Brown and her family for the comments made by the quiz-show presenter and very much regrets the embarrassment caused.

5) Laughing uncontrollably, he staggered from the room.

6) I have an eccentric cousin who insists on having exactly two hundred cornflakes for breakfast each morning, you must meet him.

7) Ben bit his lip, anxious not to say more than he should.

8) If Mr Benzie refuses to apologise, there is nothing you can do.

9) He is an idiot and no-one can deny it.

10) I need help, I need it urgently, I am desperate.

Exercise 2

Use five full stops to make sense of this carelessly punctuated paragraph. Be very careful.

I plan to get up promptly at 7 o'clock each morning, after opening all my bedroom windows and stripping my bed, I will do vigorous stretching exercises, breathing deeply, for ten minutes, I will then have a shower, dry myself briskly, and dress, breakfast will be a frugal meal, after fresh grapefruit and herb tea, I plan to jog to the town centre and back, if I can keep up this routine, and I see no reason why I shouldn't, I should be quite fit and quite slim by Christmas.

Exercise 3

Rewrite each of these sentences as two short complete statements and punctuate accordingly.

1) Although my grandfather is old, he is still very active.

2) I'll arrange for you to be transferred to Hong Kong, as you really dislike this area.

3) There's just been a news flash that there's been a terrible accident in the English Channel.

4) Cherrill thoroughly enjoyed the weekend that she spent at Pontins.

5) The rumour that the poll tax has been abolished isn't true.

Exercise 4

Restore the sentence boundaries in this extract from an article by Brian Bell printed in *The Times Educational Supplement*.

by 9.30 a.m. Wayne was already flagging tired and listless, he blinked a lot and often rubbed his hand over his face he struggled on without either interest or enthusiasm

by early afternoon the sun was shining brightly through the classroom windows Wayne sat hunched forward over his desk supporting his head in his arms as he struggled to keep himself awake by 3 p.m., head cradled in his arms, he was asleep

at 14, Wayne is one of thousands of youngsters up and down the country who spend their days in school teetering on the edge of exhaustion late nights, 24-hour television, satellite TV, the video revolution may all play a part but the most tired pupils in schools are, surprisingly, not those whose leisure pursuits keep them awake but rather those with part-time jobs which leave them tired and unable to concentrate

at 14 Wayne, with parental knowledge, begins work at 4 a.m. during the winter, if there are difficulties with snow, he may start work even earlier he is late for school most mornings after delivering milk for four or five hours and earning £3.50

while there are nowhere near as many children 'on the milk' as there are 'on the papers', there are enough to give cause for concern it is illegal for children to deliver milk at the time it is delivered but a 'blind-eye' is frequently turned on such breaches

the milk float in question is not the familiar slow battery-powered vehicle this one is a flat-bed, diesel truck and the round is big, around 300 gallons or 100 crates the boys hang on, rain, hail or shine, to the bar at the rear of the vehicle and hop off nimbly with a full bottle carrier when the truck slows

Exercise 5

Combine each of these groups of short sentences into one statement. You may change the order of the sentences.

1) Jennifer is good at mathematics. Robert prefers history.

2) We opened the door. The cottage was deserted. We felt frightened.

3) The cat scratched her ear frantically. I felt concerned. There was something wrong.

4) Few people know him well. He is shy. He is hard to get to know. He wants to be friendly. It is worth persevering.

5) Emily Bronte wrote *Wuthering Heights*. Her pen-name was Ellis Bell. She had two sisters. They wrote novels. They used pen-names.

Question marks

A sentence which is a question requires a question mark at the end of it. Note that a question mark has its own built-in full stop and the sentence will not require another one.

√ Are you coming?
✗ Are you coming?.

Note the difference between:

Are you happy?
He asked me if I was happy.

The first sentence is a **direct question**, where we are given the speaker's actual words. The second sentence is an **indirect question** (a form of statement), where a report is given of what was said. The first sentence requires a question mark; the second sentence requires a full stop.

Exercise 6

Rewrite the following indirect questions as direct questions. Punctuate carefully.

1) He wondered if I would like to appear in 'Neighbours'.

2) She asked me why I was three hours late.

3) I was asked for my name and address.

4) He questioned my sincerity.

5) I asked him what he was going to give me for Christmas.

Exercise 7

Rewrite these direct questions as indirect questions.

1) 'Can you hear me at the back?' the speaker asked the audience.

2) 'Have you tidied your bedroom yet, Matthew?'

3) 'Are you allergic to penicillin?', Dr Jones asked, looking over his glasses at his new patient.

4) 'Can you give me a hand on Sunday demolishing my garage?' my neighbour inquired.

5) 'Will you marry me, Kate?' whispered Mike.

Exercise 8

Ten of these sentences are direct questions. Write them out, correctly punctuated.

1) He asked me if I had a large spanner he could borrow.

2) Have you got a large spanner I can borrow.

3) I wonder if you would be interested in our special offer.

4) Can I interest you in our special offer.

5) What is the time.

6) She asked me the time.

7) I couldn't believe she would wear that hat.

8) Are you going to wear that hat.

9) I asked him where he was going on holiday.

10) Where are you going on holiday.

11) Do you know the answer or are you bluffing.

12) I challenged him directly as to whether he knew the answer or was merely bluffing.

13) I asked if he were certain.

14) Are you certain.

15) We don't know why she left so suddenly.

16) Why did she leave so suddenly.

17) We questioned him closely as to his motives.

18) Why did you behave as you did.

19) Was it snowing when you left Newcastle.

20) I wonder if it was snowing when he left Newcastle.

Exercise 9

Use full stops and question marks where appropriate.

1) It is so cold for July

2) May I ask how you know my name

3) Will you be paying by cheque

4) Am I taller than you

5) Isn't that my pen

6) I wonder if my parents will be coming

7) I've finished my homework

8) Do you remember meeting Robert at the concert

9) I have to go to the dentist on Monday

10) How do you do

Exercise 10

Advertisements are often written in a deliberate punchy style that flouts all the conventions of traditional sentence construction and punctuation.

1) In pairs, rewrite the text of this advertisement in full sentences, correctly punctuated. (Your version will be longer than the one here.)
2) Compare the two versions. Which do you consider makes the more persuasive appeal? Why?

Ever considered buying a villa in Spain? Because you should. And now. Property's cheap. Cheaper than you think. If you've an eye for a good investment. And this is where we come in. Write to us now. Without delay. Today not tomorrow. We'll rush you details. Of *your* dream house. All prices. Varied locations. We handle the legal side. Interested?

Exclamation marks

Exclamation marks should be used very sparingly indeed or they become tiresome to the reader and their effectiveness is lost. There are four cases which we shall look at in a moment when exclamation marks must be used. In all other cases, it is worth asking yourself (when tempted to use an exclamation mark for emphasis) whether it is really necessary. Surprisingly often, you will find that it is not needed at all and that the sentence is quite capable of speaking for itself. Keep exclamation marks in reserve for occasions when their special note of urgency is needed.

Mind that child! Stop, thief! Call the police!

It is exclamations that need exclamation marks, not every command or heartfelt statement. Note that the following sentences are sufficiently emphatic without exclamation marks.

1) I vow I will never touch a cigarette again.
2) Time yourself carefully in Paper One.
3) You are the most marvellous man I have ever met.
4) Clean your teeth thoroughly after each meal.
5) I wish I could have my life all over again.

Here are the four instances where you must use exclamation marks.

Emphatic commands

'Be quiet at the back there!' yelled the irate teacher.

Vehement wishes

'God bless you, ma'am!' breathed the starving woman.

All brief expressions of strong feeling

Hear! Hear!	(agreement)
Help!	(panic)
Ugh!	(disgust)
Hooray!	(joy)
Good heavens!	(astonishment)

Note: If the brief expression is part of a longer sentence, then there are two ways of punctuating it.

Good heavens! We didn't recognise you!
Good heavens, we didn't recognise you!

Remember than an exclamation mark, like a question mark, has its own built-in full stop. Whatever follows must begin with a capital letter.

Exclamatory sentences

An exclamatory sentence beginning in one of three following ways always requires an exclamation mark at the end.

What a . . . !   (What a lovely day!)
What . . . !   (What big teeth you have!)
How . . . !   (How brave of you!)

You have to distinguish between **exclamatory sentences** beginning with *how* and *what* and **questions** beginning with *how* and *what*, so do pay attention to the sense.

What is your name? What a name!
How clever is she? How clever!

Exercise 11

Punctuate these sentences appropriately, by using full stops, question marks and exclamation marks.

1) You should be careful to keep doors and windows locked

2) Look out

3) What have you done

4) How long it is

5) How long is it

6) I do enjoy horror films

7) We are delighted that you are back with us

8) I'm on fire

9) What a terrible moment

10) How ridiculous

11) I thought she asked you what you thought

12) How did you know what to do

13) How clever of you to know what to do

14) I feel very sorry for Pauline

15) What a marvellous morning

16) Stand and deliver

17) What very loud music

18) I asked her if she knew the answer

19) Do you know the answer

20) Sit down immediately

Exercise 12

Punctuate this extract from Christopher Sergal's dramatised version of Harper Lee's *To Kill a Mockingbird*, using full stops, question marks and exclamation marks (and capital letters) to restore the sentence boundaries. You can check your version against Christopher Sergal's by turning to the back of the book.

Jem	Who did one thing to help Tom Robinson
Miss Maudie	His friends, for one thing, and people like us we exist, too people like Judge Taylor

	people like Heck Tate start using your head, Jem did it ever strike you that Judge Taylor naming Atticus to defend Tom was no accident that Judge Taylor might have had his reasons
Scout	S'right, Jem usually the court appoints some new lawyer – one who is just startin'
Miss Maudie	You're beginning to realise a little more to it than you thought (Pressing) whether Maycomb knows it or not, we're paying your father the highest tribute we can pay a man we trust him to do it right
Scout	Then why did he get beat
Miss Maudie	(snorting): Miss Stephanie talks nonsense maybe he didn't get an acquittal, but he got something I was sitting in court waiting, and as I waited, I thought – Atticus Finch won't win, he can't win, but he's the only man in these parts who can keep a jury out so long in a case like this. And I thought to myself, take note of this time and this place it's 1935 and it's Maycomb, Alabama, and we're making a step – it's just a baby-step, but it's a step

Chapter Two

CAPITAL LETTERS, ABBREVIATIONS, CONTRACTIONS

Capital letters

As we have established in the last chapter, sentence boundaries are indicated by capital letters at the beginnings of sentences and end stops at the ends. How many other circumstances can you recall when capital letters should be used?

Exercise 13

List the six different reasons why capital letters are used in this extract from an article printed in *The Independent*.

Greenies who deserve 1001 Brownie points

Diana Hinds gets a lesson in ecologically sound living from one of Britain's most committed couples

THE FIRST thing that Bernadette Vallely did when I arrived at her north London flat was to apologise for not offering me real milk in my tea. 'Stewart and I don't drink milk, but you could have soya or powdered.' At first I opted for no milk at all, then soya. 'It might taste funny if you've never had it before,' Bernadette warned, trying hard not to sound patronising.

Bernadette Vallely, director of the Women's Environmental Network and author of a new book, *1001 Ways to Save the Planet*, and Stewart Boyle, who works for the Association for the Conservation of Energy, are possibly one of the most 'environmentally sound' couples in Britain. Their teatime conversation revolves around the difficulties of safely disposing of fridges so that the CFCs can be recycled, and finding car-hire companies that can supply cars with catalytic converters.

'It's unbelievable,' Stewart said. 'One car-hire assistant told me, "Oh yes, all the cars are green — but I don't know if they have catalytic converters." He meant they all took unleaded petrol; he had no idea what happened to the rest of the pollution from a car. Awareness is very thin; it's very light green.'

The Independent, 5 April 1990

In addition to the six different uses exemplified above, there are other occasions when capital letters are used. In order to make quite sure that you understand each separate use, let us briefly examine each one.

Sentences

Always begin a sentence with a capital letter. This familiar rule is rather surprisingly not always observed by students! It is worth taking care with your handwriting so that small letters and capital letters are clearly distinguished. You'll probably find that some letters cause you more trouble than others, according to your handwriting style.

Exercise 14

Rewrite the following paragraph by replacing the missing full stops and capital letters.

in the long hot summer of 1921 a serious drought hit the country springs dried up, the well filled with frogs, and the usually sweet water from our scullery pump turned brown and tasted of nails although this drought was a relief to my family, it was a scourge to the rest of the village for weeks the sky hung hot and blue, trees shrivelled, crops burned in the fields, and the old folk said the sun had slipped in its course and that we should all of us very soon die there were prayers for rain; but the family didn't go, because it was rain we feared most of all.

Laurie Lee, Cider with Rosie

The pronoun 'I'

Always use a capital letter for the pronoun 'I'. There are no exceptions to this rule. The pronoun 'I' is written with a capital letter wherever it comes in the sentence. Note that the capital letter remains even when two words are run together in a contraction.

I've   I'll   I'm   I'd

Exercise 15

Read the extract below.

1) In pairs, establish where the sentence boundaries come (and notice there are two questions among the statements).

2) How often is 'I' written wrongly with a small letter?

the very first poem i remember hearing at my primary school i've always thought a masterpiece, and dearly wish i'd written it myself. it's a murder ballad; author: anon i should also tell you that i was madly in love with the infant teacher who read it to us i can see her now: tall, calm amid the smells and squalls of the baby class; a pre-Raphaelite beauty with cool marble hands and soft brown hair hanging below her shoulders.

as for the poem itself, i had no idea that – in varying European forms – it perhaps had its origins in Scandinavian myth and the death of Balder, the god of light, or that it's believed by some to be an allegorical account of the murder of William Rufus in the New Forest in the year 1100, as well as – a bit nearer our own time – an ironic tale of the end of the career, in the eighteenth century, of Sir Robert Walpole.

i enjoyed – and enjoy – the poem as a poem about the death of that bold and independent bird, the robin.

one little point about the verse:

Who'll toll the bell
i said the bull
Because i can pull . . .

how often have you seen him depicted as a farmyard bull, of massive animal architecture i'm certain we should really see a bird here, the bullfinch, for all the other animals in the poem are small ones: sparrow, beetle, fly, fish, linnet and so on.

Charles Causley introducing 'Who Killed Cock Robin?' in Radio 4's *With Great Pleasure* in 1977

Proper nouns

Always begin proper nouns with a capital letter. Proper nouns are names of particular people (Diana, Stewart, Bernadette), places (London), months (April), and so on. Common nouns are more general (person, city, month). The following list may be helpful.

Proper nouns include:
1) Christian names and forenames: Anna, Yin
2) Surnames: Fortescue
3) titles: Sir Tom Putt, Doctor Brown, Uncle Vanya, Mrs Evans.
4) countries and continents: Poland, Australia.
5) nationalities, tribes, races: Dane, Sioux, Aztecs.
6) adjectives actively derived from countries, continents, nations and races: German efficiency.
7) towns and cities: Chicago, Tokyo.
8) streets: Raleigh Road, Acacia Avenue.
9) names of houses: Merrist House, Dunroamin.
10) geographical features: Mount Everest, Mississippi River.
11) days of the week: Tuesday.
12) months of the year: February.
13) special festivals: Christmas, Easter.
14) historical periods: the Middle Ages, the Renaissance.
15) organisations: Women's Environmental Network, Royal Society for the Protection of Birds (RSPB).
16) companies: The Ideal Laundry.
17) political parties: the Freedom Party.

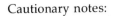

Cautionary notes:

1. Use lower case letters for seasons of the year (**spring, summer, autumn, winter**).
2. School subjects generally do not need capital letters (**biology, chemistry, history**) but language subjects do (**English, French, Latin**).
3. If the national connection has been lost in the mists of time, drop the capital letter (**brussels sprouts, venetian blinds, french windows**).
4. Sometimes the use of a capital letter is optional: We stood as the bishop (**Bishop**) entered.
   BUT
   We stood as the **Bishop of Chichester** entered.

In those cases where you can exercise your own discretion (and inclination), it is worth being consistent or the reader is made uneasy.

Exercise 16

25 additional capital letters are required in this exercise.

1) My favourite day of the week is thursday and my favourite subject is geography.

2) We are studying the effects of the industrial revolution on the rural community.

3) I was born in portsmouth but moved to the channel islands before I started school.

4) The present queen of england is queen elizabeth.

5) I remember mrs brown telling me years ago that harriet wanted to be an industrial chemist when she grew up.

6) My mother is learning spanish this winter.

7) The entire owen family struggled to the summit of cader idris.

8) The ombudsman advised me to write to the prime minister myself.

9) On wednesday, march 9th, the twins were born.

10) The course is sponsored by the council for the preservation of rural england.

Religion

Always use a capital letter when referring to God, or the names and titles of God. (**God, the Persons of the Trinity, the Holy Trinity, the Father, the Son, the Holy Spirit, the Saviour, the Almighty, the Messiah, the Lord, Allah, Yahweh,** etc.)

A capital letter is also used when referring to sacred books (**the Bible, the New Testament, the Old Testament, the Qur'an, the Pentateuch,** etc.)

Religions are also given capital letters (**Christianity, Buddhism, Hinduism**), as are believers (**Christians, Buddhists, Hindus**).

- Pagan gods are not given capital letters.

    It was Neptune, god of the sea, who summoned up the storm that drowned the sailors.

    Neptune, of course, has a capital letter because that is his name but god doesn't have one.

- It is correct to use capital letters for personal pronouns and possessive adjectives referring to God but in recent years it has become less usual.

Let us praise God.   Let us praise **Him**.
Let us praise **His** ways. √
Let us praise God.   Let us praise him.
Let us praise his ways. √

Either form is correct. It is important to be consistent, however, to avoid making the reader uneasy.

Exercise 17

Use capital letters where they are needed.

1) Blessed be god for ever.

2) Who was the Greek god of war?

3) The bible is not so widely read now as it once was.

4) God the father, god the son, and god the holy spirit are the three persons of the holy trinity.

5) We shall study in turn christianity, judaism, buddhism and islam.

Titles

Use a capital letter at the beginning of the first word of a title, the last word, and all the most important words in between.

We all enjoyed reading *A Day in the Life of a Mouse.*
Have you seen *A Room with a View?*
I read it in *The Independent.*

Exercise 18

Use 20 capital letters where they are needed in these titles.

1) We shall be reading *a village by the sea*.

2) Is anyone else auditioning for a part in *an inspector calls*?

3) I saw the advertisement in today's copy of *the daily telegraph*.

4) The producer decided to call the programme *the rise and fall of the smoking habit*.

5) Do you listen to *the archers* every day?

6) I should like to order two copies of *mathematics for the general student*.

7) My brother saw *jaws* ten times.

Poetry

Capital letters are usually used at the beginning of each line of poetry. An example should make this clear:

> **O** that 'twere possible,
> **A**fter long grief and pain,
> **T**o find the arms of my true-love
> **R**ound me once again!
>
> Alfred Lord Tennyson, 'Maud'

Some poets (e.e. cummings, for example) deliberately take liberties with capital letters and they should be quoted accordingly.

> i thank You God for most this amazing
> day for the leaping greenly spirits of trees
> and a blue true dream of sky; and for everything
> which is natural which is infinite which is yes
>
> e.e. cummings, 'i thank You God'

Exercise 19

Use capitals where necessary in this poem by William Blake.

> never pain to tell thy love
> love that never told can be
> for the gentle wind does move
> silently, invisibly.
>
> i told my love, i told my love,
> i told her all my heart,
> trembling, cold, in ghastly fears –
> ah, she doth depart.
>
> soon as she was gone from me,
> a traveller came by,
> silently, invisibly –
> he took her with a sigh.

Direct speech

Direct speech (a quotation of the actual words of a speaker) always begins with a capital letter wherever it occurs in a sentence.

> She said, 'We will come if we possibly can.'
> 'We will come if we possibly can,' she said.
> 'We will come,' she said, 'if we possibly can.'

Structurally the sentence within the inverted commas is quite self-contained. It may help to remember that it is *a sentence within a sentence* and needs its own capital letter.

Note: There is a section on the punctuation of direct speech later in the book. There are other pitfalls!

Exercise 20

Use capital letters where necessary in the following conversation. (Five are needed.)

The small boy looked very tearful. He muttered, 'must I go to bed?'

'you must go to bed,' his mother replied, 'and you must go now.'

He pleaded, 'all my friends go to bed at midnight.'

His mother's patience was exhausted. She lifted him clumsily and marched towards the stairs.

'put me down,' he sobbed. 'put me down!'

Letters

Notice the use of capital letters in the letter layout below.

9 Willow Crescent,
Cosham,
Portsmouth,
Hants PO9 2EX

6 April, 1990

Dear Mr Askew,

       Your letter arrived ....

....

....

       With any luck ....

....

       Yours sincerely,
       Gladys Taber

Note particularly:

- The use of capital letters in the address and the postcode.

- The use of a capital letter with the **first** word in the salutation. Had the salutation been longer, the first word only would need to be capitalised (apart from any names, of course.)

Dear Mr Askew
My dear Mr Askew
My very dear Mr Askew

- The use of a capital letter with the first word in the body of the letter, even though it follows a comma after 'Dear Mr Askew'.

- The use of a capital letter with the **first** word of the complimentary close. (It is a common error to use capital letters for each word at this point.)

Yours sincerely √
Yours faithfully √
Your loving nephew √

Exercise 21

Use 40 capital letters where necessary in the letter that follows. (This exercise will be useful for revision.)

rose cottage,
6 the green,
friary park,
cheshire sk8 2ey

monday, 20th august

dear john,

we all enjoyed reading your letter. what a marvellous holiday in the united states you must have had! we all envy you horribly.

is there any chance that we may see something of you at easter? do let us know if you can manage to spend a few days at least with us.

fiona got good grades in all her 'a' levels, i am glad to say, and she's now sure of her place at queen mary college (that's london university). her geography result was better than we expected.

we're off on holiday next saturday for three weeks on the isle of wight. we had to book our passage on the car ferry way back in march!

with every best wish,
alison

Entire words in capitals

Writing a word in capital letters can suggest the emphasis you would give that word in conversation. This is a device appropriate to informal writing rather than to formal writing.

In the extract below George MacBeth is discussing Rachel Lindsay's poem 'The Congo':

> The headlong flood of the rhythm will pretty quickly get a grip on you. Feel the surge and bang of the words as you read them aloud. Aloud, because this is not a poem which will yield up much interest if quietly mouthed over in a hushed monotone, or murmured only for the inner ear. It needs to be YELLED.
>
> George MacBeth, *Poetry for Today*

Capitals in headings

Be alert to the use of capital letters in printed material: newspaper lay-outs, advertisements, reports, leaflets, magazines, contents pages, etc. Typographically there are many styles of capital letters and a huge range in presentation is possible. The visual implications can be very exciting.

Exercise 22

In groups or pairs discuss the typographical presentation and lay-out of this extract from Geraldine Pettigrew's 'Proposals for the English Curriculum'. Consider the size and appearance of the typefaces as well as the functions of the capital letters.

Levels 8, 9 and 10

What will be expected at Levels 8, 9 and 10 is highly competent expression, good organisation, a flair in the handling of language, and a consistent personal style.

LEVEL 8

ATTAINMENT TARGET

The ability to make and shape text in order to communicate meaning in written language, appropriate to context, purpose, reader or audience.

The characteristics of performance which indicate that pupils have attained Level 8 will include the ability to:

(i) **produce writing which has material selected appropriately for the purpose and reader; writing in a form, structure and style which is uniformly competent;**

(ii) **produce a piece of writing, based on research, sustained to an appropriate length;**

(iii) **review and revise their own writing effectively as a result of their own analysis.**

LEVEL 9

ATTAINMENT TARGET

The ability to make and shape text in order to communicate meaning in written language, appropriate to context, purpose, reader or audience.

The characteristics of performance which indicate that pupils have attained Level 9 will include the ability to:

(i) **produce writing which shows perception, and is organised and handled with confidence;**

(ii) **demonstrate consistently a developed personal voice;**

(iii) **demonstrate an assured awareness of match between text and reader;**

(iv) **demonstrate that length, structure and layout is appropriate to task.**

LEVEL 10

ATTAINMENT TARGET

The ability to make and shape text in order to communicate meaning in written language, appropriate to context, purpose, reader or audience.

The characteristics of performance which indicate that pupils have attained Level 10 will include the ability to:
- (i) consistently demonstrate striking and memorable writing;
- (ii) demonstrate an ability to create writing across a range of styles and forms, and an ability to initiate their own forms on occasions;
- (iii) demonstrate the ability to organise complex or demanding subject matter in an assured and highly competent fashion.

Exercise 23

In pairs or small groups, study the front page of any tabloid newspaper. Locate the whole words, phrases and sentences that have been printed in capital letters.

a) List the different purposes for which such capitalisation has been used (main headline? caption to photograph? etc.).

b) How many typographical forms of capitals have been used?

c) Range them in order of visual impact, the most striking first.

Abbreviations and contractions

MRS T MOST UNPOPULAR PM IN HISTORY!

MRS THATCHER is now the most unpopular Prime Minister in the history of opinion polls.

Fewer than one in four of those questioned in the latest Gallup poll said they were satisfied with her performance.

And Tory hopes of winning the next General Election are sinking along with their leader's popularity.

The poll puts Labour 24.5 per cent ahead of the Tories – the biggest Labour lead recorded by Gallup since the pioneers of polling began.

Labour has been more than 20 points ahead only twice before.

And on both occasions – in 1963 and 1971 – it went on to win the next election.

The plunge in Mrs Thatcher's popularity . . .

Daily Mirror, 6 April 1990

The above extract from the *Daily Mirror* makes use of universally understood abbreviations in its headline:

MRS T MOST UNPOPULAR PM IN HISTORY

Let us look now at the conventions governing abbreviations and contractions. You will see that sometimes the initial letter of key words are used, sometimes the first and last letters, sometimes the first part of a word, and so on. It is important to use the accepted abbreviated form. Some dictionaries list abbreviations and contractions in an appendix.

Words and phrases are abbreviated according to a number of conventions.

Mrs. T.	(**Missis** **T**hatcher)
P.M.	(**P**rime **M**inister)
G.C.S.E.	(**G**eneral **C**ertificate of **S**econdary **E**ducation)
Dr.	(**D**octo**r**)
etc.	(**etc**etera)
approx.	(**approx**imately)
Cpl.	(**C**or**p**ora**l**)

● Note that capital letters only are used in the abbreviated form of some words and phrases:

CFCs (**C**hloro**f**luoro**c**arbons)
P.T.O. (**P**lease **t**urn **o**ver)

● Similarly some abbreviated forms are *never* written in capital letters.

e.g. (**e**xample **g**iven)

● Capital letters can also usefully distinguish two forms:

P.M. (**P**rime **M**inister)
p.m. (**p**ost **m**eridiem = after noon)

You may already have noticed in your general reading as well as in your reading of the text above that sometimes full stops are used to indicate abbreviations and sometimes they are not. It has actually been perfectly acceptable for some time to omit the full stops in such abbreviations as Mr, Mrs, Dr, Rd, where the word has been shortened to its first and last letters.

√ Mr. Brown
√ Mr Brown

However, modern typing practice (and printing practice too, as you can see in this book) is to omit full stops with all abbreviations and this is having its effect, although more slowly, on hand-written practice also. It may be wise to continue to use full stops with abbreviations in handwritten work for a little longer if you are preparing for external examinations. Some examining boards are more traditional in their practice than others.

On the other hand, it is interesting to note that two very modern additions to our vocabulary are *never* used with full stops in their abbreviated form: CFCs and plc.

Have a close look at a few different newspapers and periodicals to see where they print BBC or B.B.C., Mrs Thatcher or Mrs. Thatcher, 17 Oct or 17th Oct., am or a.m. This will indicate the general trend.

CAUTIONARY NOTES BEFORE WE PASS ON TO CONTRACTIONS

- If your sentence ends with a full stop indicating an abbreviation, you won't need another one to show that the sentence is finished. The single full stop will do double duty.

  √ **We met promptly at 7 p.m.**
  ✕ **We met promptly at 7 p.m..**

- Items in a list of abbreviations must, of course, be separated by commas in the usual way whether full stops have been used to indicate the abbreviations or not.

  In a remarkable career, Sir Mark Genius has been Chairman of the B.B.C., the C.B.I., I.C.I., and British Rail.

- Do take care when you use the abbreviation **etc**. It's a lazy device in most cases and is usually better avoided, but if you must use it, spell and punctuate it correctly.

  √ **etc**
  √ **etc.**
  ✕ **e.t.c.**
  ✕ **e.c.t.**

Words and phrases can be shortened in a less drastic way than in the abbreviations we have just been examining. If just a few letters are omitted, an apostrophe is used to show where this has happened.

In some contractions, two words are combined into a new form and an apostrophe indicates the missing letters.

it's	(it is/it has)
who's	(who is/who has)
he'd	(he had/he would)
they're	(they are)
you've	(you have)
isn't	(is not)
don't	(do not)
wouldn't	(would not)
didn't	(did not)

● Be very careful with the placing of the apostrophe. Its function is to indicate the omitted letter or letters, not to show where the two words have been joined. In some words the apostrophe *appears* to perform this second function but do not be misled or you may begin to use the apostrophe in the wrong place with contractions incorporating 'not'.

  √ didn't   ✕ did'nt
  √ wouldn't ✕ would'nt

Apostrophes are also used:

● In shortened words and phrases

  o'clock (of the clock) – never used in its full form now!

● In poetry to enable the line to scan

  The boast of heraldry, the pomp of pow'r,
  And all that beauty, all that weath e'er gave,
  Awaits alike th' inevitable hour:
  The paths of glory lead but to the grave.

                Thomas Gray, 'An Elegy in a Country Churchyard'

- In mispronounced words when first or last letters are omitted

  'Arry's bin thinkin' an' thinkin'.
  'E's 'ad a 'ard time in 'arrow.

- In dates where the century is understood

  I left South Africa in '76.

- In certain rare adjectival constructions

  I always was a poor, weak, one-idea'd creature.

  Mrs Yeobright in Hardy's *The Return of the Native*

  Usually one adds *-ed* to a noun used adjectivally like this but after a vowel it would look ugly.

- In plurals of abbreviations

  Only ten M.P.'s were present.

- In plurals of letters, numbers, and symbols

  Dot your i's and cross your t's.
  Form your 6's and 9's more carefully.
  Write the △'s and □'s in red.

- To avoid confusion

  It is best not to use so many 'but's'.

Exercise 24

Use 20 apostrophes where necessary

1) Ive forgotten his name but its on the tip of my tongue.

2) Hes been worrying so much that hell fail this examination.

3) Theyve said theyre coming at nine oclock.

4) Ang your at on the ook in the all.

5) Well be leaving Exeter in 98.

6) Its a great pity youve not met before.

7) The terraced garden and the japonicad porch looked beautiful.

8) "The sunshine is a glorious birth:
   But yet I know, whereer I go,
   That there hath passd away a glory from the earth."

9) Alls well that ends well.

10) Youre absolutely right.

Exercise 25

Use apostrophes where necessary (15 altogether).

1) You had better mind your ps and qs when Aunt Emily comes to stay.

2) For many years the 3Rs have been much neglected.

3) N.C.O.s are asked to report immediately.

4) In the 1960s everything was so much cheaper.

5) Take care with bs and ds; they are easily confused.

6) The ◊s and △s signify women and girls.

7) They've ordered ten JCBs.

8) The under-12s will benefit from the new legislation.

9) Sheila always uses continental 7s.

10) I always enjoy writing capital Qs.

11) Your ys and js are too similar.

Exercise 26

20 apostrophes are needed here.

1) He doesnt expect to pass the examination and hes thoroughly depressed.

2) Dont go too near the edge of the platform.

3) Its quite natural for a monkey to eat bananas.

4) Whos been using my toothbrush?

5) Im sure its more difficult than he says.

6) At ten oclock everyones going to be rushing for the Liverpool train.

7) Theyre both very hardworking and Im quite sure theyll both get As.

8) Hell do you credit.

9) Were anxious to canvass everyone in the area.

10) You shouldnt use pencil for this kind of work.

11) Its been a long time since theyve visited London.

12) Your father wont recognise you after all this time now that youve lost all your teeth.

Before we leave contractions and abbreviations, let us briefly examine some commonly confused homophones:

IT'S and ITS
WHO'S and WHOSE
THEY'RE, THEIR, THERE
YOU'RE, YOUR

Even if you have a word processor with a spelling check, you won't find it much help with these, so let's sort them out now.

IT'S and ITS

IT'S (contraction = **IT IS/IT HAS**
It's been a long term.   (=It has)
It's not fair.   (=It is)

ITS (possessive adjective (like **HIS**))
The dog wagged **its** tail.
Don't judge a book by **its** cover.

Exercise 27

It's or its?

1) . . . very kind of you.

2) I know . . . overdue.

3) The cat waves . . . tail with venom.

4) . . . been snowing all day.

5) He claims . . . a question of principle.

6) Edward says . . . at the bottom of the lake.

7) The car has had . . . engine completely overhauled.

8) . . . echoes could be heard all over York.

9) . . . always been his ambition to stand for Parliament.

10) . . . a long lane that has no turning.

Exercise 28

It's or its?

1) . . . never too late to learn to punctuate.

2) There's a sting in . . . tail.

3) You could see . . . tracks all over the garden.

4) And there the snake shed . . . skin.

5) . . . too good to be true.

6) What's . . . weight?

7) . . . entirely up to you.

8) My watch has lost . . . second hand.

9) That elastic has lost . . . stretchiness.

10) . . . always raining.

WHO'S and WHOSE

WHO'S (contraction) = **WHO IS/WHO HAS**
Who's there? (=Who is)
Who's been smoking in here? (=Who has)

WHOSE (relative adjective)
The driver **whose** leg was amputated has had to take early retirement.

WHOSE (interrogative adjective)
Whose disgusting shoebag is this?

Exercise 29

Who's or whose?

1) . . . coming with me?

2) Mr Cooper is a man . . . teaching skills are well known.

3) . . . books are these?

4) The farmer . . . haystacks were destroyed is not insured.

5) Gary doesn't yet know . . . able to come.

6) . . . the Brain of Britain?

7) . . . writing is this?

8) I don't know . . . more nervous, the cast or the audience.

9) The winner . . . entry was correct won £5.

10) . . . been using my hairbrush?

THEY'RE, THEIR, THERE

THEY'RE (contraction) = **THEY ARE**
They're coming up the drive. (= They are)

THEIR (possessive adjective) = **belonging to them**
The twins have lost **their** cat.

THERE (adverb of place)
I'll drive you **there**.

THERE (impersonal adverb)
There is no point in coming.
There are all sorts of possibilities.

Exercise 30

They're, their or there?

1) . . . coming to stay for the weekend.

2) My aunt and uncle are selling . . . car.

3) I hope . . . not serious.

4) . . . addicted to 'Neighbours', as far as I can see.

5) . . . is no objection as far as the committee is concerned.

6) Have you been . . . before?

7) I know . . . furious with you.

8) . . . are blackfly all over the runner beans!

9) Remember that . . . are two sides to every argument.

10) My parents are so set in . . . ways.

Exercise 31

You're or your?

1) . . . not serious, are you?
2) Everybody agrees that . . . the best person for the job.
3) Could I borrow . . . pen for a moment?
4) . . . sister has lost a lot of weight, hasn't she?
5) I like . . . boyfriend.
6) . . . always so calm!
7) . . . tax demand is on the kitchen table.
8) I hope . . . in a good mood before I tell you the news.
9) . . . shoes need mending.
10) . . . absolutely right.

Chapter Three

COMMAS

There are nine different circumstances in which you should use commas, and a number of other circumstances where you are free to use your own judgement and discretion. We will examine each of these in turn, with exercises as we go. At the end of the section there will be mixed practice exercises on the use of commas. Remember that there must always be a reason for using **any** punctuation mark; it is not a random affair. Rather than disrupt the flow of a sentence with too many commas, modern practice has moved towards economy in such matters. Do not omit the compulsory ones, but be sparing with the optional ones.

Lists

Commas are used to separate items in a list. This is one of the most familiar of all the uses of the comma.

> **I bought bacon, eggs, mushrooms, bread and coffee.** (list of nouns)

> **Kay is pretty, intelligent, kind and popular.** (list of adjectives)

> **We coaxed, bribed, threatened and finally used physical force.** (list of verbs)

> **I plan to do the washing, slip down town, have lunch and then renew my car insurance.** (list of statements)

Look at this splendid list of names taken from marriage licence documents 1685–1851 by Mr John Rayment.

The commas make it quite clear how many people are being named by keeping each set of names distinct.

● Incidentally, it is quite correct (despite what you may have been taught when you were younger) to use a comma before 'and' in a list. Indeed, there are occasions when you must do so to avoid confusion. Look at this sentence.

The four firms concerned were Smith and Stephens, Boultons, Tuckers and Kays and Jones.

If you are not familiar with the names of the firms, it is quite impossible to be sure of the names of the third and fourth firms in the list.

1st firm – **Smith and Stephens**
2nd firm – **Boultons**
3rd firm – **Tuckers? Tuckers and Kays?**
4th firm – **Kays and Jones? Jones?**

Just one comma is needed to make all clear, and, since the purpose of punctuation is to make your meaning clear to your reader, you must use a comma here before 'and'.

1) The four firms concerned were Smith and Stephens, Boultons, Tuckers, and Kays and Jones.
2) The four firms concerned were Smith and Stephens, Boultons, Tuckers and Kays, and Jones.

There are those who would recommend always using a comma with 'and' so that this kind of confusion is automatically avoided. They would also claim that there is another advantage in using a comma with 'and': the last two items are kept apart by the comma and there is no suggestions that there might be a special connection between them.

Read the two pairs of examples below. Which sentence in each pair do you prefer?

We bought flour, raisins, cooking oil, bread and butter.
We bought flour, raisins, cooking oil, bread, and butter.

For breakfast we had sausages, mushrooms, eggs, baked beans and bread and butter.
For breakfast we had sausages, mushrooms, eggs, baked beans, bread, and butter.

Remember that, unless it is essential to avoid confusion, the use of a comma before 'and' is a matter of personal taste.

Exercise 32

Read this news item from *The Independent* and look closely at the commas used in each of the three paragraphs. Which of these statements is correct?

Commas are used to separate items in a list in:

a) each of the three paragraphs
b) the first paragraph only
c) the first and second paragraphs only
d) the first and third paragraphs only

Conquered by the Classics

THEY came, they saw, they were conquered. A report by HM Inspectors on "Effective Learning and High Standards in Classics" fairly bubbled with enthusiasm for what they found in the classrooms of 20 schools in England.

Clear objectives, high expectations, mutual respect and teachers setting examples of scholarship and intelligent involvement indicated that something is definitely going right.

The custodians of learning added: "It was at times exhilarating to observe the confidence and excitement with which pupils drew on previous experiences to develop cognitive strategies for acquiring new learning." Sounds Greek but, we believe, this is HMI-speak for a very good lesson.

The Independent, 5 April 1990

Exercise 33

Restore the commas needed to separate items in lists in these extracts from *First Steps in Counselling* by Ursula O'Farrell.

a) Posture nervous movements inability to relax inappropriate laughs or smiles all these can indicate the emotional state of our clients more accurately than spoken words.

b) Perhaps one of the hardest parts of listening, in the counselling setting, is dealing with silences. In our everyday conversations, silences rarely occur, and, when they do, are often causes of embarrassment. We hurry to fill the gap we search frantically for a phrase or topic to re-start the conversational engine which has stalled we even have phrases such as 'angels passing' or 'someone walking on my grave' to cloak the quiet moment to drown the silence. In the counselling setting, silences can be seen in a different light as they can be most productive if handled correctly.

c) The client's recording of events or reactions is the main clue we have about the situation which is causing difficulty or unhappiness. This recording sets the scene fills in the background and reflects how the client sees the situation how he chooses to describe it and how much he wishes to reveal.

Exercise 34

Restore the commas needed to separate listed items in these extracts from *Stress and Relaxation* by Jane Maddens.

a) The 'fight or flight' response is important for all animals when life is threatened, but we are unlike them in that we can produce these physical and chemical changes for situations that do not require vigorous physical activity. A car driver fuming at traffic delays a mother exasperated by her children frustrating committee meetings being late for an appointment a row with a boss an income-tax demand may all produce the same response as those for a threat to life.

b) Individuals experiencing temporary fear joy aggression or grief will convey messages to other people by their posture. Sometimes these postures are transferred to others: in a research project to assess the posture of schoolchildren, it was found that where the school principal was dominating aggressive and feared by the children the majority of them had round backs as did many of the teachers. Where the school principal was brisk and alert and the atmosphere was of eager activity, many of the children had hollow backs.

Asides

Commas are used to mark off short asides. Some examples will illustrate this point.

> Children are very demanding, **I quite agree**.
> **Well,** I'm sorry.
> Could you pass the gravy, **please**.
> You've met Terry O'Leary before, **haven't you**?

Exercise 35

Put commas around the asides in the following sentences:

1) His behaviour I regret to say has been deplorable.
2) As you will know there is very little that can be done.
3) It's a nice recipe isn't it?
4) In fact the outcome was quite different from what we had expected.
5) To put the story in a nutshell he packed his bags and was gone by the morning.
6) I hope or rather I expect to see him next Sunday.
7) Please can you help me?
8) Children love sandy beaches don't they?
9) In conclusion the Chairman thanked all members of the Committee for their hard work throughout the year.
10) He knew however that he could get home in time.

Addressing people

Commas are used to mark off names of people spoken to. This use of commas is very similar to the last one. Here are some examples of commas marking off names. Notice a pair of commas is sometimes needed.

'Your Honour, I am guilty.'

'Good morning, **Mrs Jones**.'
'**Margaret**, can you spare a moment?'
'I think, **Mrs Cooper**, that it would be best to say no more!'

Terms of address, such as **sir, madam, ladies and gentlemen**, are punctuated in the same way.

'**Your Honour**, I am guilty.'
'Please bear with me, **ladies and gentlemen**, while we adjust the microphone.'
'Can I help you, **madam**?'

Exercise 36

Use commas where they are needed.

1) 'Good morning Mr Evans. Do come in.'

2) 'Yes my love. You are quite right,' he murmured.

3) 'I am quite convinced Upper 3 that you can do better than this,' said Mrs Hayman.

4) 'Anna and Matthew supper is ready!'

5) 'Mrs Thompson you're quite a stranger!'

6) I object most strongly sir to the tone of yesterday's editorial.

7) 'Doctor do come in.'

8) 'Are we ready ladies?' asked Canon Green gently.

9) 'Ladies and gentlemen our speaker has been delayed.'

10) 'Karen I should like you to meet Miss Holborn.'

Phrases in apposition

A pair of commas is used around a phrase in apposition.
Consider these two sentences:

> **Prince Charles was married in 1981.**
> **The Queen's eldest son was married in 1981.**

These two statements could be combined very easily.

> **Prince Charles, the Queen's eldest son, was married in 1981.**
> **The Queen's eldest son, Prince Charles, was married in 1981.**

Prince Charles and **the Queen's eldest son** refer to the same person and are grammatically interchangeable. Whichever phrase you put second is said to be in apposition to the first. Take care to enclose the phrase in apposition with a pair of commas if it occurs mid-sentence. It is a very common error to omit the second comma.

Exercise 37

Use commas around the phrases in apposition.

1) I wish my boyfriend Matt Streat had not had his ear pierced.

2) Do you know the Lord Mayor Edward Hallett personally?

3) Sonia Blackheath the Chancellor of the Exchequer has resigned.

4) Everyone loves our two cats Blackie and Sooty.

5) Graham Green's biographer Norman Sherry will be autographing copies of Volume 1 in Dillons on Thursday.

6) My best friend Mary has an off-beat sense of humour.

7) In her case, it's no coincidence that her fiancé Louis Cooper happens to be rich.

8) The occasion her parents' golden wedding anniversary was a splendid excuse for a grand family reunion.

9) Isca Water a newly privatised company has had tremendous problems with pollution.

10) I will have you know that my son your husband has never been spoilt at any time of his life.

Participles

Commas are used to mark off phrases beginning with participles. Don't let the term **participle** alarm you. Here are some examples of phrases beginning with participles being marked off by commas from the rest of the sentence.

> She hesitated, **looking wistfully around the room.**
> **Walking nervously towards the house,** she once again rehearsed what she had to say.
> (*Looking* and *walking* are both present participles.)
> The fox, **hunted remorselessly to its death,** never had a chance.
> **Beaten though they were,** the first eleven felt quite pleased with their efforts.
> (*Hunted* and *beaten* are both past participles.)

These phrases which offer additional information are very much like asides; they are separate from the main structure of the sentence. You will 'feel' this if you read the examples aloud, pausing at the commas.

● Note that the first comma should be placed immediately before the participle.

√ She knocked at the door one last time and then, **shrugging her shoulders**, turned away.

✗ She knocked at the door one last time, and then **shrugging her shoulders**, turned away.

As a double check, the sentence should read smoothly if the phrase between the commas is omitted.

● Be careful not to omit the second comma of the pair. It is easily done.

Exercise 38

Place commas where they are needed to mark off these participial phrases.

1) She paced around the room biting her fingernails anxiously.

2) Subdued at last the tiger slept.

3) Celia posted the letter and then putting the matter entirely out of her mind strode away.

4) Not believing in miracles any more I must accept my fate.

5) Refusing help the old man slowly made his way home.

6) The young husband dried the last plate and placing it with the others in the china cupboard smiled smugly.

7) Exhausted by the long wait for the bus they sank into the upholstered seats gratefully.

8) The headmaster questioned both lads watching their reactions very shrewdly.

9) Sipping her sherry Deirdre at last made up her mind.

10) Mr Brown's secretary slipping quietly into the office passed her employer a large sealed envelope.

Adverbial clauses

Commas are sometimes needed with subordinate adverbial clauses. Look at these two sentences.

> **Although he was very tired,** he walked all the way home.
> He walked all the way home **although he was very tired**.

A comma is not needed in the more straightforward second sentence where the main clause comes first and the subordinate clause follows.

In the first sentence we have the subordinate clause first. The slight pause that the comma affords alerts the reader to the importance of the main clause which follows.

If the subordinate clause is placed in the middle of the main clause then a pair of commas is needed.

> He walked, **although he was very tired,** all the way home.

Exercise 39

Use commas only where they are essential.

1) As he was tired Shaun decided to go home early.

2) Shaun decided to go home early as he was tired.

3) Shaun decided as he was tired to go home early.

4) Mr White is retiring early because he is not in the best of health.

5) Because he is not in the best of health Mr White is retiring early.

6) If you accept our invitation to come for Christmas we shall all be delighted.

7) He paid his debts although he was not very happy about it.

8) When Matthew sat the entrance examination he was very nervous at first.

9) Wherever you go you will see the same thing.

10) Unless you complain officially about the noise nothing will be done.

11) At last Mr Wilson agreed that if the doctor insisted he would take a holiday.

12) As her boyfriend was behaving so abominably Lydia decided to give him up.

13) Amelia spring-cleaned the flat while her flat-mate was away.

14) I always open the window as soon as I get home.

15) After she posted the letter she started to cry.

Adjectival clauses

Commas are used with non-defining adjectival clauses. Look at these two sentences. The use of a comma can affect the meaning quite dramatically.

Kate went to the disco with her boyfriend, who has red hair. Emma went to the disco with her boyfriend who has black hair.

Who has more boyfriends currently, Kate or Emma?

The comma provides the vital clue.

Kate went to the disco with her boyfriend, **who has red hair**.

The words in bold type qualify the word 'boyfriend' and offer the sort of additional information that could be bracketed or even omitted as far as her friends are concerned. (They would all know that her boyfriend has red hair.) Kate clearly has one boyfriend (is not two-timing him) and this non-defining adjectival clause tells us **more** about him. **Use a comma,** as you would for an aside.

Emma went to the disco with her boyfriend **who has black hair**.

Here the words in bold print tell us more about her 'boyfriend' but they don't give us extra information which could be omitted rather, they supply vital information **which identifies which boyfriend Emma was with that evening**. This defining adjectival clause .**defines**. **Don't use a comma.** (A pause would ruin everything.)

Exercise 40

Commas are needed in four of the sentences below:

1) I go to the hairdresser who has a salon on the corner of the Parade.

2) The children who wanted ice-cream queued at the left-hand counter; the children who wanted lemonade queued at the right-hand one.

3) The house which is one of the nicest in the road has belonged to my aunt for thirty years.

4) Have you read the book that everyone is talking about?

5) This hat which I bought in a jumble sale two years ago is my husband's favourite.

6) The shop which is run by a dragon of a woman never has anything in stock that anybody wants.

7) The boy who was making a nuisance of himself was warned by the policeman who had dealt with him before.

8) Do you know the lady who has moved next door?

9) The twins who were suntanned and relaxed had just got back from the Canary Islands.

10) The lorry which had been belching fumes all the way from London finally broke down when it reached Guildford.

Direct speech

Commas are used in the punctuation of direct speech. Look carefully at how commas have been used in these three sentences.

'I am appalled,' she said, 'at your behaviour.'
'I am appalled at your behaviour,' she said.
She said, 'I am appalled at your behaviour.'

A comma marks the change from speech to narrative and from narrative to speech each time. Sometimes other punctuation marks are used as you will see in the section on inverted commas but the general point can be made now that some form of punctuation is **always** necessary.

Exercise 41

Use commas where they are needed (10 altogether).

1) 'I've missed the bus again,' moaned Louise.

2) The little girl said wistfully, 'We've never been abroad.'

3) 'Christmas won't be Christmas without any presents,' grumbled Jo.

4) 'I very much regret,' said the headmaster, 'having to announce that the school will be closed all next week while asbestos is being removed from the corridors.'

5) The policeman took out his notepad and said, 'Can you give me full details of what happened as you turned the corner, madam?'

6) 'I'm sorry to interrupt your conversation,' said Miss Brewster, 'but there has been an urgent telex from Hong Kong.'

7) 'Don't forget to lock the back door when you go out,' said Alan's mother, 'and make sure nothing is left switched on.'

Pauses

Commas are used to mark a pause in a long sentence. Personal taste (within reason) dictates very largely where these commas should be placed. For example, it *does* help to read the sentence below aloud and to see where you would pause in speech. Long sentences do not necessarily require commas but in practice the reader is often helped by them.

Georgette Heyer made a point of not re-reading *Vanity Fair* while she was writing *An Infamous Army*, and when she did turn to it afterwards she was shocked at Thackeray's lack of research as revealed in his assumption that the gunfire of the battle could be heard in Brussels.

Jane Aiken Lodge, *The Private World of Georgette Heyer*

Exercise 42

Use just one comma in the best possible place to introduce a pause in this long sentence.

We decided we would try to get tickets for the final performance of 'Swan Lake' at the Royal Opera House in three weeks' time although we knew in our heart of hearts that we had very little chance of success at such short notice.

Exercise 43

Read the following passage carefully to yourself. At which two or three points might a comma prove helpful?

The unexpected news of his death stunned the family and all who knew him partly because he had been so exuberantly fit and healthy for his age and partly because he had been so full of plans for this first year of his retirement. Over three hundred grieving friends and relations packed the village church for the funeral service and mourned him in an eloquent silence which was broken only by the stifled sobs of his grey-haired daughters and by the poignantly full-throated birdsong in the trim churchyard. He was later quietly and sadly laid to rest in a sunny corner of the tiny graveyard in his beloved village in his adopted county of Devon as he would have wished.

The remaining uses of the comma are also very much a matter of personal style and preference. Let us now look at these discretionary uses.

Optional uses of the comma

Letter lay-outs

Most handwritten letters are laid out traditionally and most typed letters are fully blocked, but both forms are acceptable for both handwritten and typed letters.

Exercise 44

Study the two examples which follow and in pairs discuss the differences in punctuation, positioning and paragraphing between the two lay-outs.

Traditional layout

8 Long Bank Road,
PENZANCE,
Cornwall,
PE5 9AB

31st August, 1991

The Managing Director,
Thomas Tackers Ltd,
PLYMOUTH,
Devon,
PL2 8TS

Dear Sir,

It is now some weeks . . . .

. . . .

I had hoped . . . .

. . . .

In the circumstances . . . .

. . . .

. . . .

Yours faithfully,

Anne Prior (Mrs)

Note: 1) Use a comma, if you wish, after house number.
2) Substitute a full stop for the comma, if you wish, after 'Cornwall' and 'Devon'.

Fully blocked layout

8 Long Bank Road
PENZANCE
Cornwall
PE5 9AB

31 August 1991

The Managing Director
Thomas Tackers Ltd
PLYMOUTH
Devon
PL2 8TS

Dear Sir

It is now some weeks ....
....

I had hoped ....
....

In the circumstances ....
....

Yours faithfully

Anne Prior (Mrs)

Note: 1) The writer's address and the date can be placed in
          the top right-hand corner but is kept 'blocked' as
          here and not sloped.
       2) The recipient's address can be put at the foot of the
          letter, after the signature, but is kept on the left-
          hand side.

Exercise 45

This letter from *The Times* is set out slightly differently again to suit the format required on the Letters Page.

1) Copy out the letter, setting it out according to the traditional layout form

2) Copy out the letter, setting it out according to the fully blocked form.

Note: You will need the address of *The Times*:

1 Pennington Street, LONDON E1 9XN

Assume the date is 16 June 1991.

Metaphorical mix-up
From Mr Eric Chisholm
Sir, Could I offer a further contribution to the list of mixed metaphors (letters, June 6, 10, 14, 17)?

After years of indecision on a council project, the chairman of the relevant local authority committee encouraged the members to more positive action by reminding them that they had stood on the edge of a precipice for far too long – it was time to take a major step forward!
Yours faithfully,
ERIC CHISHOLM,
33 Willow Road,
Charlton Kings,
Cheltenham, Gloucestershire.

The Times

To avoid confusion

Earlier in this section, we noticed that the comma has sometimes to be used with 'and' in a list to avoid confusion. There are often situations involving 'and' where the reader must be protected from making the wrong connections.

> Last Friday I drove ten miles to see my aunt and my fan-belt broke.

There is a possibility that the reader will momentarily assume that you planned to see your aunt and your fan-belt. He will hesitate when that doesn't make sense and tackle the sentence again. A comma after 'aunt' would have avoided the confusion because it clarifies meaning. Anticipate any possible misinterpretation by your reader and punctuate considerately.

Here is another example:

> The wine-glass had been left on the terrace. It was empty and full of red ants crawling excitedly in the stickiness.

There is an uneasy moment when the reader learns that the glass is empty and full at the same time. A comma after 'empty' removes any difficulty.

Number

Modern mathematical practice is to leave a small space instead of the comma when writing out a large number.

> 1 760 000 = 1,760,000

Emphasis

A comma, since it invites the reader to pause momentarily, helps to give emphasis to what follows. On the occasions where such emphasis is required, a comma can be used at a point in the sentence where it would not normally be used.

> **He accepted my offer, quickly.**

Out of context, we cannot understand why he accepted the offer so quickly but that he did so is made very clear by the comma.

Practice exercises

Straightforward exercises are followed by more demanding
ones at the end.

Exercise 46

15 commas are needed in the following sentences. Some
sentences can be left as they are.

1) Henry an experienced cyclist found the route com-
   paratively easy.

2) Although we had very little to offer them we felt we
   had to invite them to stay for supper.

3) Nobody knows if it was ever found again.

4) Harriet insisted however that there was nothing
   wrong.

5) James asked 'What are we having for supper tonight
   Mum?'

6) I have packed Wellington boots plimsolls sandals
   walking-shoes flip-flops and slippers.

7) Overcome by emotion she sobbed.

8) 'Good morning everyone. Do sit down' intoned Mr.
   Weaver.

9) Before I answer that question I should like to make this
   further point.

10) The stamps which have faulty perforations may be
    worth a lot of money. (Not all the stamps have faulty
    perforations.)

Exercise 47

Use commas where required in the following sentences.

1) Anna plays the piano guitar descant recorder treble recorder and flute.
2) I must apologise ladies and gentlemen for the delay in starting.
3) My neighbour Mrs Greenham is a delightful person.
4) 'We're going on holiday next week' said Mrs Prince.
5) Laughing uncontrollably Christine ran out of the classroom.
6) 'We haven't got any cotton-wool in stock' said the shop assistant apologetically.
7) If you insist on washing up I shall feel obliged to help.
8) Jane's mother who is extremely house-proud washes her dustbins every week.
9) Madam there must be some mistake.
10) Crouched close over his work Stephen peered through thick-lensed spectacles.

Exercise 48

Insert commas where needed. (20 essential commas, 2 optional ones.)

1) The kitten a beautiful tabby was quite enchanting.
2) Yes I do agree with you Simon.
3) Belfont House which is open to the public every day except Christmas Day is well worth seeing.

4) If you are free on Tuesday let's go together.

5) I hear moreover that he is a very selfish man.

6) We have visited Italy Greece France Spain Norway and Sweden in the last five years.

7) The school which is a co-educational comprehensive has a splendid reputation.

8) Bent double under the weight the slave staggered forward.

9) 'You must know' he said 'that we are all relying on you.'

10) Already today I have written five letters tidied the house weeded the strawberry bed and prepared lunch.

Exercise 49

Punctuate the following, using commas, full stops, question marks, exclamation marks and capital letters where necessary.

1) have you met my mother-in-law Mrs Allen

2) what a frightful experience for you all

3) 'now we shall never know' mr cobley said in conclusion 'whether the treasure a priceless collection of precious stones was ever on board the *santa veronica*'

4) help

5) the friend who has helped me most since i have been ill is my next-door neighbour brenda carter

6) cauliflower cabbage brussels sprouts and purple-sprouting broccoli should be planted now

7) as they rounded the bend they saw the horrifying sight before them

8) smiling nervously william shook mr thorpe's hand

9) did you see all the instalments of *brideshead revisited*

10) 'sugar' the old lady exclaimed

Exercise 50

Use commas where necessary. (18 essential commas, 4 optional ones.)

1) 'I know' said John Brown 'that you will have a lot to say to each other.'

2) Mrs. Jackson despite her earlier objections is now quite happy with the scheme.

3) The chess team from my school has played ten matches has lost five won three and drawn two.

4) The bird a fledgeling had been badly mauled by the cat.

5) Although Louise rarely refers to her childhood I believe she had a very unhappy time at home.

6) Miranda's house was sold in fact within six weeks.

7) Mr. Brown Gary's been sick.

8) The trip to Brighton was exhausting expensive time-consuming and a total disaster.

9) The group of students whispering softly moved slowly around the cathedral.

10) Jennifer will consider the venture very carefully before committing herself will need to discuss the details with her accountant and will be in touch with you in about a fortnight.

11) The instructions were clear concise and helpful.

Exercise 51

1) Add commas where you think they are needed to this paragraph from Anita Brookner's *Look at Me*.

2) In pairs, justify the decisions you have made. (Remember your version may differ from your partner's where optional commas have been used.)

3) Turn to the back of the book, and compare your version and your partner's version with the original punctuation. Would you now wish to modify the way you punctuated the passage or do you prefer your version to Anita Brookner's one?

'But first of all we must do something about your appearance' Alix would say and this meant sitting me down at her dressing table and dabbing at me with blushers and eye shadows and then turning me round and showing me to Nick. He would reward me with his hard speculative gaze which brought more colour to my cheeks although when I was turned round again to inspect myself in the mirror I would be horrified to see my clean brown face so smudged and as I watched my new slightly crooked dark red lips utter some words I was quite surprised that my new enlarged eyes could register such pain. I became quite firm on the matter of my appearance and wiped and scrubbed all the colour off raising my dripping face in their bathroom to find Nick leaning curiously against the door jamb. I would brush past him and go back into the bedroom to do my hair only to find Alix at her dressing table turning her head from side to side to study the back of her neck anchoring her chignon with pins and combs settling her pearly studs in her ears and stubbing out her cigarette. Myself quite forgotten.

Exercise 52

Read the extract from *Solitude* by Anthony Storr and then answer the questions that follow.

Modern psychotherapists, including myself, have taken as their criterion of emotional maturity the capacity of the individual to make mature relationships on equal terms. With few exceptions, psychotherapists have omitted to consider the fact that the capacity to be alone is also an aspect of emotional maturity.

One such exception is the psychoanalyst, Donald Winnicott. In 1958, Winnicott published a paper on 'The Capacity to be Alone' which has become a psychoanalytic classic. Winnicott wrote:

It is probably true to say that in psychoanalytical literature more has been written on the *fear* of being alone or the *wish* to be alone than on the *ability* to be alone; also a considerable amount of work has been done on the withdrawn state, a defensive organisation implying an expectation of persecution. It would seem to me that a discussion on the positive aspects of the capacity to be alone is overdue.

In Chapter 1, I referred to Bowlby's work on the early attachment of the human infant to its mother, and to the sequence of *protest, despair,* and *detachment,* which habitually occurs when the infant's mother is removed. In normal circumstances, if no disastrous severance of the bond between mother and child has occurred, the child gradually becomes able to tolerate longer periods of maternal absence without anxiety. Bowlby believes that confidence in the availability of attachment figures is gradually built up during the years of immaturity; more particularly during the period from the age of six months to five years, when attachment behaviour is most readily elicited. However, sensitivity to the presence or absence of attachment figures continues until well into adolescence. Many middle-class English children who had experienced total security in early childhood have had their expectations rudely shattered when sent to boarding school at the age of seven or eight.

Solitude, Anthony Storr

1. Why has a pair of commas been used around 'including myself' (para 1)?
2. Why is there a comma after 'psychoanalyst' (para 2)?
3. Is it true or false to say that the main function of the comma in the sentence starting 'It is probably true . . .' (para 3) is to introduce a pause in an otherwise long sentence?
4. Why has a comma been used after 'despair' (para 4)?
5. How would the meaning of the sentence be altered if a pair of commas was used to enclose 'who had experienced total security in early childhood' (para 4)?

Chapter Four

INVERTED COMMAS

Inverted commas are also known as **speech marks** and **quotation marks**. Their use around quotations and titles is dealt with later in this section. It is their use in the punctuation of direct speech (words actually spoken) that presents most difficulty. We shall therefore deal with the punctuation of speech in some detail.

Direct speech

The four sentence patterns of direct speech. There are four sentence patterns in direct speech as far as punctuation is concerned.

- **Speech first, narrative second**
  'We are off to London tomorrow,' she said.

- **Narrative first, speech second**
  She said, 'We are off to London tomorrow.'

- **One sentence of speech interrupted by narrative**
  'We are off,' she said, 'to London tomorrow.'

- **Two or more sentences of speech divided by narrative**
  'We are off to London tomorrow,' she said. 'Cross your fingers it doesn't rain. We don't want to have to take macs and umbrellas.'

When you want to punctuate direct speech in your own writing, you should be able to match what you want to punctuate with one of the patterns above.

To make absolutely sure that you can 'teach yourself' from these patterns, we can look at each a little more closely.

Speech first, narrative second

Look at these examples:

> 'Your ears are very large,' she said.
> 'Aren't your ears rather large?' she asked.
> 'What large ears you have!' she exclaimed.

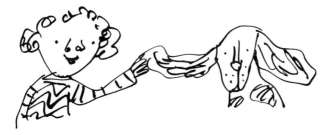

- There is **always** a punctuation mark marking the transition from speech to narrative. Only the three punctuation marks used above can be used at this point in this sentence pattern.

- The inverted commas enclose both the words spoken **and** the punctuation mark that goes with them.

- A small letter is used at the beginning of *she asked* and *she exclaimed* even though one follows a question mark and the other follows an exclamation mark because the sentence as a whole has not yet been completed.

Exercise 53

Punctuate these sentences using the examples above as a guide.

1) have you always been a vegetarian the young reporter asked.

2) you need a haircut said his mother bluntly.

3) how dare you say i'm fat Shaun's young sister cried.

4) Kate has failed her driving test again whispered Becky discreetly to the waiting friends.

5) Ian goes back to America on Friday Anna told us glumly.

Narrative first, speech second

Look at these examples:

> **She said, 'Your ears are very large.'**
> **She asked, 'Aren't your ears rather large?'**
> **She exclaimed, 'What large ears you have!'**

- There is always a comma in this sentence pattern marking the transition from narrative to speech.

- The inverted commas enclose the words spoken **and** the end stop (either full stop, question mark or exclamation mark). The one end stop marks the end of the direct speech and the end of the sentence as a whole in this pattern.

- Notice the first word of direct speech begins with a capital letter. Think of the words spoken as being a sentence in their own right and it won't seem so illogical.

Exercise 54

Punctuate these sentences using the examples above as a guide.

1) The invigilator said calmly stop writing now

2) Claire smiled at the stray cat and whispered would you like some milk

3) Both parents said together no, you can't go to the fair

4) The young man said here is my pedlar's licence

5) Mr MacBean hesitated and then asked despairingly how do I know that you are telling the truth

Interrupted narrative

One sentence of speech interrupted by narrative.

> 'I have no intention,' she said firmly, 'of giving you another penny!'

This pattern puts together the two patterns we have already examined but note that **of** begins with a small letter, because the sentence of direct speech has not yet ended.

Exercise 55

Punctuate the following sentences using the example above as a guide.

1) does anybody want to buy a ticket Alison shouted for the Jason Donovan concert in Birmingham

2) if you haven't got your science overall with you snapped the irate chemistry teacher then you won't be doing science today

3) before the matinee announced Mrs. King we'll have a picnic lunch in Covent Garden

4) i've been dieting now for four weeks pouted Claire and I've lost only half an ounce

5) why don't you have supper with us suggested Matthew and then let me run you home

Interrupted speech

Two or more sentences of speech divided by narrative.

The example we had earlier was:

> 'We are off to London tomorrow,' she said. 'Cross your fingers it doesn't rain. We don't want to have to take macs and umbrellas.'

Notice how one pair of inverted commas encloses all the speech before the narrative and one pair encloses all the speech that follows. You *don't* need inverted commas around every sentence. Inverted commas simply signify to the reader where the speech begins and where it ends.

Exercise 56

Add inverted commas, commas, full stops and capital letters. Note that there are two spoken sentences each time.

1) thank you so much for your help said mrs greenham it has been much appreciated

2) i am sorry that you are leaving us said juliet quietly i do hope you will like the new job

3) it's difficult to be sure about what happened the police constable said we shall have to investigate further

4) we shall begin with some revision exercises miss jones said in the second half of the lesson i shall want to start something new

5) i'm going in now said john it's too cold for gardening today

6) the children have washed up the breakfast things announced their father now they're going to hoover the sitting room

7) i'm off to bed now smiled ann-marie i've got to be up early in the morning

8) when you've both finished your homework you can play for a little while their mother said i want you in bed by nine o'clock

9) we apologise for the loss of your picture announced anna ford meanwhile we shall have some music

10) your letter came yesterday said the woman it was a great relief

Exercise 57

Add inverted commas where they are needed.

How long have you had Snowy? asked Aunt Gladys.

We were given him about five months ago, answered her nephew. A friend of mine asked if we could take him over. He said he would gladly give us the hutch and a supply of oats and hay. We thought about it for a bit and then said we'd love to have him.

Do rabbits need a lot of attention? asked his aunt.

No. They're really very easy pets, he said. I clean Snowy's hutch out once a week. I feed him once a day and, whenever it's sunny, I let him out of his hutch and he scampers around the garden.

Does he eat the vegetables?

I chase him off!

He's a dear little thing, smiled Aunt Gladys. Perhaps I ought to get a rabbit too.

Dialogue

Spacing is important in the punctuation of dialogue.

● Take a new line for a new speaker, and indent.

● Take a new line for the resumption of the main narrative, and indent.

I was taken into a Form Room and told to sit at a desk. All the other boys were out of doors, and I was alone with the Form Master. He produced a thin greeny-brown covered book filled with words in different types of print.

'You have never done any Latin before, have you?' he said.

'No, sir.'

'This is a Latin grammar.' He opened it at a well-thumbed page. 'You must learn this,' he said, pointing to a number of words in a frame of lines. 'I will come back in half an hour and see what you know.'

Behold me then on a gloomy evening, with an aching heart, seated in front of the First Declension.

Mensa	a table
Mensa	O table
Mensam	a table
Mensae	of a table
Mensae	to or for a table
Mensa	by, with or from a table

What on earth did it mean? Where was the sense in it? It seemed absolute rigmarole to me. However, there was one thing I could always do: I could learn by heart. And I thereupon proceeded, as far as my private sorrows would allow, to memorize the acrostic-looking task which had been set me.

In due course the Master returned.

'Have you learnt it?' he asked.

'I think I can *say* it, sir,' I replied; and I gabbled it off.

He seemed so satisfied with this that I was emboldened to ask a question.

'What does it mean, sir?'

'It means what it says. Mensa, a table. Mensa is a noun of the First Declension. There are five declensions. You have learnt the singular of the First Declension.'

'But,' I repeated, 'what does it mean?'

'Mensa means a table,' he answered.

'Then why does mensa also mean O table,' I enquired, 'and what does O table mean?'

'Mensa, O table, is the vocative case,' he replied.

'But why O table?' I persisted in genuine curiosity.

'O table,—you would use that in addressing a table, in invoking a table.' And then seeing he was not carrying me with him, 'You would use it in speaking to a table.'

'But I never do,' I blurted out in honest amazement.

Winston Churchill, *My Early Life*

© Curtis Brown on behalf of the Estate of Sir Winston Churchill

Exercise 58

Punctuate and set out correctly the following extract from *Across the Barricades* by Joan Lingard. You can check your version against the original by turning to the answers in the back of the book.

the dog who was sitting on the garden path, saw her first and got up with a welcoming bark mr blake looked up from his weeding sadie anything wrong no he came to the gate you dont look your usual bouncy self its just that ive got the sack and mrs mcconkey is dead mrs mcconkey kept the shop near us i see i wanted someone to talk to so i thought i'd come and see you come in they sat in the kitchen sadie rested her folded arms on the kitchen table we always used to make fun of mrs mcconkey she sighed we would shout names at her when we were small and run like blazes before she get hold of us she never did because she was too fat and now shes dead aye its bad sadie theres no denying it scarcely a day goes by without somebody getting killed but when its a person you know its not so easy to take its not easy at all said sadie

Exercise 59

There is a punctuation error in each of the following sentences. Write out each sentence correctly punctuated. (Look carefully at commas, inverted commas, full stops, question marks, exclamation marks and capital letters.)

1) 'I think I'll go now', said Mrs Jones.
2) 'You know very well,' answered my mother 'that I always answer letters.'
3) 'I'm delighted that you can come' smiled Mrs Thompson.
4) 'Am I late,' asked Nicola?
5) The twins said, 'all our friends get more than fifty pence a week pocket money.'
6) 'Is anyone at home?' Called the milkman.
7) 'Sophie has passed English language.' boasted her proud mother.
8) Mr Bennet retorted immediately 'Well, in that case, you can walk!'
9) 'Help!' Cried the drowning man.
10) 'This exercise is not so easy as I thought' commented Lydia.

Exercise 60

Punctuate this extract from *The Silver Sword* by Ian Serraillier. You can compare your version when you have finished with the original by turning to answers at the back of the book.

theres been a mistake and ive come to explain said ruth in polish this is jan its all his fault i want to speak for him the interpreter translated who is the other child said captain greenwood my sister bronia said ruth she has nothing to do with this but i had to bring her along as i had nowhere to leave her were on our way to switzerland and are camping by the mill-stream i see whats the boy's full name said captain greenwood only jan – thats the only name of his we know said ruth jan have you any parents said captain greenwood the grey cat and jimpy but they're dead and ruths my mother now said jan sullenly captain greenwood could make nothing of this ruth did her best to explain a situation she did not fully understand herself we take it then that you have no parents but that this young lady ruth balicki aged eighteen sister of edek balicki is your guardian said captain greenwood.

Exercise 61

Punctuate:

what do you feel are your main weaknesses miss meloy asked i know my spelling is pretty awful and i'm always making punctuation mistakes replied geoffrey you need plenty of practice then his teacher said that can be arranged easily enough are you prepared to do extra homework i am very willing replied geoffrey

Exercise 62

Punctuate:

1) i mustnt forget to buy more flour muttered aunt elsie.

2) it is never too late said mr wilkens firmly to learn to punctuate

3) uncle fred asked james quietly do you know what has happened to your garden shed

4) i promise that youll have a square meal this evening smiled their mother well have roast chicken with two vegetables followed by chocolate pudding and cream will that satisfy you

5) excuse me have you lost your purse no i havent but thank you for asking

Exercise 63

Punctuate this extract from *In Custody* by Anita Desai. You can check your version with the original printed at the back of the book.

will you print my poems if i send them to you – the remaining ones in the sequence no who wants to read your poems murad said at once abruptly i have enough poems for the issue already as soon as i sent out the circular announcing it contributions started pouring in poems poems poems everybody writes them i tell you he complained plucking at his hair in mock distress

Titles and Quotations

- Use inverted commas around titles of books, newspapers, magazines, comics, films, radio programmes, television programmes. (In print, however, these usually appear in italic type without the inverted commas as in this book.)

> I saw the advertisement in 'The Times'.
> (I saw the advertisement in *The Times*.)
> 'Star Trek' was a great commercial success.
> (*Star Trek* was a great commercial success.)

- Use inverted commas around quotations.

> 'Keep up your bright swords, for the dew will rust them' is a splendid example of Othello's elevated language.

- Inverted commas are also used around particularised words and phrases.

> I don't think 'conceited' really describes him at all.
> I am not yet 'into' antiques.
> He is a very 'avant-garde' young painter.
> How do you spell 'achievement'?

Single or double inverted commas?

It is for you to choose whether you use single (' ') or double (" ") inverted commas. Either form is correct. It is important, however, to be consistent.

Some people reserve double inverted commas for punctuating direct speech and single inverted commas for all the other occasions when inverted commas are required. This can be a useful distinction. (In print, however, this style might be reversed.)

> She asked, "Have you ever read 'Pride and Prejudice'?"
> He said slowly, "Did I hear you say 'I have no intention of taking the examination'?"

Exercise 64

Enclose all the titles with inverted commas. (Not every sentence contains a title.)

1) Antony and Cleopatra and Romeo and Juliet are the two Shakespeare texts we shall be studying.
2) The whole class enjoyed The Mill on the Floss.
3) I must read the whole of Tennyson's In Memoriam.
4) Prince Hal finally has to reject Falstaff and his friendship.
5) Do you read The Sunday Times or The Observer?
6) I am replying to your advertisement in last night's Evening Express.
7) Hamlet is usually portrayed as a pale-faced young man in black velvet.
8) I don't read Dandy any more now that I'm ten.
9) Panorama will be screened later this week.
10) Anna Karenina was a splendid film.

Exercise 65

In pairs, discuss the use of inverted commas in the following extract from an article published in *The Sunday Times*.

Mixed-up mongrels make work for pet psychiatrists

As the British pet population grows, so do the queues at the pet psychiatrists, or 'pet behaviour consultants' as they prefer to be called.

'People have lost their ability to communicate with their dogs,' explains John Rogerson, who runs a clinic in Co.

Durham. 'People have become much more selfish, and just as they find they have increasing problems in communicating with each other, so it is with their pets.'

David Appleby, who runs Dog Help, a mobile service in the Midlands, reckons one in five dogs has a behavioural problem. Most problems with dogs, he says, are related to aggression, directed at owners, other humans or other dogs.

But 'separation anxiety', which can lead to dogs destroying the home, howling and losing control of their bodily functions, is another common reason for referral.

Most behavioural difficulties, the psychiatrists believe, stem from a conflict of concepts. The owner takes a parental role, treating the dog as a wilful child. But the dog views the people he lives with as part of his pack. Problems are most common where a dog feels he is the dominant member of the pack. A human who threatens this dominance is met with aggression.

For example, an estimated 85% of attacks take place in the bedroom, when the owner tries to go to bed. From a puppy, a dominant dog has become accustomed to taking the best place to sleep.

Dominant dogs learn the rules of dominance in three other areas of activity while in the litter: grooming, feeding and playing. It is the dominant puppy which gets groomed by the others, is fed first and gets to keep the rag doll.

'Dogs are often fed first, allowed to sleep on the master's bed while the master never sleeps in the dog's place, always get groomed and always gets to keep the toys. No wonder they feel they are dominant,' explains John Fisher, of Greengarth Clinic in Bookham, Surrey.

Part of his treatment of dominant dogs involves the owner standing in the dog's basket so the dog realises who is the master. Other therapies involve the owner taking all the toys away and bringing them out only under his control. After play, they are locked away again — as a way of indicating who is in charge.

Hugh Thompson

© *The Sunday Times*, 28 May 1989

Chapter Five

POSSESSIVE APOSTROPHES

There is a simple rule for knowing where to put the possessive apostrophe, and a complicated one which most people remember inaccurately as ' 's in the singular and s' in the plural'.

I'll deal with the complicated rule first because so many people have been taught it at one time or another and have been confused by it ever since that they might like to sort it out before considering the easy rule.

Complicated rule

Singular nouns require **'s** in all cases.

  the **man**'s beard
  the **dog**'s bowl

Plural nouns which form their plural by adding s (or a suffix ending in s) require **s'**.

  the **dogs**' bowl
  the **ladies**' voices

Plural nouns which form their plural by adding a suffix not ending in s or which undergo internal change require **'s**.

  the **men**'s laughter
  the **children**'s footsteps
  the **women**'s votes

There is a much simpler rule which I have found is very easily applied by all students. It avoids the singular/plural issue altogether and you don't have to choose between 's and s'. (That sorts itself out automatically.)

Simple rule

Place the apostrophe immediately after the name of the 'owner':

the **man**'s beard (= the beard of the **man**)
the **men**'s laughter (= the laughter of the **men**)
the **dog**'s bowl (= the bowl of the **dog**)
the **dogs**' bowls (= the bowls of the **dogs**) '
the **ladies**' changing rooms (= of the **ladies**)
the **women**'s changing rooms (= of the **women**)

Use whichever of the two rules you prefer. Either rule, correctly applied, will mean you put the apostrophe in the right place every time.

Exercise 66

Rewrite in a form which requires an apostrophe.

For example: the smile of a mother

a mother's smile

1) the questions of the pupils

2) the response of the audience

3) the roar of the crowd

4) the hop of a frog

5) the fragrance of the flowers

6) the enthusiasm of the boy

7) the bright dresses of the women

8) the voices of the policemen

9) the evidence of the witnesses

10) the tail of the mouse

Examine carefully any mistakes which you made in Exercise 66. Make sure you understand where you went wrong before attempting Exercise 67.

Exercise 67

Rewrite in a form requiring the apostrophe.

1) the antennae of the butterflies

2) the paw of the cat

3) the waiting room for ladies

4) the games of children

5) the headlights of the car

6) the hands of the clock

7) the wigs of the footmen

8) the decision of the manager

9) the wife of the ambassador

10) the wives of the aldermen

● If you add 's to a singular noun already ending in -s, you are adding a syllable to the pronunciation of that word.

the **princess's** slipper (princess's = 3 syllables)
the **ass's** bray (ass's = 2 syllables)

- It is permissible to drop the -s, if wished, in the possessive form of PROPER nouns only.

  Keats's poetry/**Keats'** poetry
  (2 syllables)   (1 syllable)

  Both forms are correct. In practice, many people *write* the longer form but *say* the shorter one.

  Usage dictates some forms. It must be **St James's Park** in London, for instance, in both speech and writing.

- Many expressions to do with time require an apostrophe.

  A **day's** work
  five **weeks'** holiday
  a **year's** absence
  a **moment's** hesitation

- Remember that sometimes the second noun (particularly 'shop' or 'house') is understood but not stated.

  I'll buy some cough mixture when I go to the chemist's.
  (i.e. chemist's shop)
  Are you going to Jo's tonight? (i.e. Jo's house)

  Note:
         ✗ He is a friend **of my father's.**
  Either: √ He is a friend **of my father.**
  or: √ He is **my father's friend.**

Exercise 68

Use apostrophes where necessary. (Some sentences will not require any.)

1) Joan Perkins is the brides sister.

2) After a moments thought he shook his head.

3) The firm of Pinder and Tuckwell is a well-established ladies and gentlemens outfitter.

4) The Members Tent was overcrowded as usual.

5) The complaints of the parents were taken quite seriously by each form mistress.

6) The childrens toys were scattered all over the floor.

7) Mr Briggs adores gentlemens relish.

8) The princesses suitors were called in one by one.

9) Have you read Jan Morriss latest novel?

10) The Citizens Advice Bureau will be able to help.

Exercise 69

Use apostrophes where necessary.

1) Mr Harriss son is the brides first cousin.

2) I will tell you how the plan works in a years time.

3) Why not join the Booklovers Club?

4) I must apologise for the piles of clothes and books on all the chairs.

5) The workmens response to the crisis was magnificent.

6) The Headmasters Conference strongly criticised the report although it was accepted by the Teachers Union.

7) He visited every builders merchant in the town.

8) The childrens doctor had found nothing wrong.

9) It is all in a days work.

10) There are blackberries at the bottom of her garden and weeds in mine.

Exercise 70

There are five deliberate errors in the use or omission of the possessive apostrophe in the following passage. In pairs, identify the five errors and then check your findings with the answers in the back of the book.

Mrs Hodge, for heavens' sake sit down and relax. Have you met John's aunt, Mrs Moss? Of course, I was forgetting, Muriel's daughter introduced you at the Adamsons party. Yes, isn't she overpowering! One of lifes leaders. Too true. She's President of the Philatelists' Club, Chairman of the Townswomens' Guild, Vice Chairman of the Birdwatchers Circle and Secretary of the Disabled Children's Society. She's never at home, you know. She's always on the go, never a moment's peace. Not really one of my friends though.

Exercise 71

Five possessive apostrophes have been omitted from this article from *The Sunday Times*. In pairs decide where the five missing apostrophes are needed. Check your version with the original at the back of the book.

Davys lamp loses its spark

Miners are worried that the governments Health and Safety Executive is planning to replace the Davy lamp, their historic symbol, with a "less accurate" electronic meter.

They say draft plans to sweep away laws that give Nacods, the pit deputies union, control over safety in the pits will also mean the lamp being replaced with an electronic methanometer — what miners call the "electric canary".

The Davy lamp was invented by Sir Humphry Davy in 1815 to trace lethal, odourless methane gas. The first lamp was tested on New Years day, 1916, at Hebburn Colliery, Tyne and Wear. An updated version of the lamp is still in use.

Experts say the new monitor, which looks like a cricket umpires light meter, can read methane levels with an accuracy and speed that the Davy lamp cannot.

© *The Sunday Times,* 16 April 1989

Chapter Six

COLONS AND SEMI-COLONS

Colons (:) and semi-colons (;) were once used far more extensively than they are today. See how in one short sonorous verse from the 1611 Authorised Version of the Bible there are two colons and one semi-colon.

But take heed to yourselves: for they shall deliver you up to councils; and in the synagogues ye shall be beaten: and ye shall be brought before rulers and kings for my sake, for a testimony against them.

(1611) *Authorised Version*

In the New International Version, this single sentence from Mark 13:9 becomes three sentences requiring no other punctuation but capital letters and full stops.

You must be on your guard. You will be handed over to the local councils and flogged in the synagogues. On account of me you will stand before governors and kings as witnesses to them.

NIV Study Bible, 1987

Colons and semi-colons do, however, still have useful functions in our plainer, more direct, twentieth-century style.

Colons

- Colons can be used very effectively to introduce lists. It would not be wrong to use a comma instead but the impact of the colon would be lost. The experienced reader knows, for example, when he sees the colon after *ingredients* in the following sentence that those ingredients are going to be itemised.

  You need the following ingredients: eggs, butter, flour, sugar and milk.

- Colons are very often used in the punctuation of dialogue in plays.

  Scout: The Tom Robinson case must be pretty important. Atticus (speaking quietly): It goes to the essence of a man's conscience.

  (*The Play of 'To Kill a Mockingbird'*, dramatised by Christopher Sergel)

- Some writers use a colon before direct speech (instead of a comma) in narrative.

  To my amazement, I heard Mary say: 'I am never coming back.'

- Make sure when using a colon to introduce a list that it has been preceded by a 'summing-up' word or phrase.

  Mr Fletcher raised the following objections : the scheme was difficult to implement, it was unfair to younger candidates, and it was likely to prove expensive.

  I bought all the equipment I needed : snorkel, fins, rubber suit, hood and weight-belt.

Exercise 72

Replace commas by colons where appropriate.

1) I think I have remembered everything, string, nails, plywood, hammer and pliers.

2) Do pack all the toilet gear you require, shaving brush, razor, toothpaste, toothbrush, soap, shampoo and deodorant.

3) All my tools were stolen from the boot, jack, foot pump, spanners, levers and tyre gauge.

4) All the paraphernalia of home-dressmaking lay spread around her, scissors, thread, pins, french chalk, pattern pieces, seam binding and buttons.

5) As I struggled for breath in the water, the main events of my life seemed to pass before my eyes, my miserable childhood, my grammar-school days, those halcyon years at university, marriage, children and now this!

6) I must insist you follow these instructions to the letter, go straight there, speak to no one on the way, leave the moment the meeting is over and return here as quickly as you can.

7) You can use this pesticide with all the brassicas, broccoli, sprouts, cabbage and spring greens.

8) Every single item of cutlery was stolen, knives, forks, dessert spoons, dessert forks, serving spoons, serving forks and all the teaspoons.

9) Judith enjoys all school subjects, Latin, French,

English, maths, physics, chemistry, biology, geography, history and divinity.

10) We visited some literary shrines, the Brontë vicarage at Haworth, the churchyard at Stoke Poges, Jane Austen's cottage at Chawton, Gilbert White's rectory at Selbourne and, of course, Stratford.

Exercise 73

Colons have been wrongly used in five of these sentences. Can you identify the errors and correct them?

1) Here are: apples, pears, plums, gooseberries and bananas.

2) We picked a huge bunch of flowers: daffodils, tulips, irises and hyacinths.

3) We visited: Brussels, Paris, Rome, Lisbon and Seville.

4) I felt threatened by the pile of bills in my letter tray: a gas bill, an electricity bill, a rate demand, a telephone bill and a repair bill.

5) I shall never forget his advice: 'Be pleasant to everyone and trust nobody.'

6) We looked at the contents of his pockets arranged neatly on the desk top: sweet papers, a chewed rubber, matches, string, a grubby handkerchief and the catapult.

7) She planned: to clean the living room, to write her letters and to do an hour's gardening.

8) All the furniture was neatly stacked: chairs, tables, wardrobes, beds and kitchen cupboards.

9) We have many birds in the garden at the moment: blue-tits, great-tits, chaffinches, siskins, robins and blackbirds.

10) Jane Austen wrote six novels: *Sense and Sensibility*, *Pride and Prejudice*, *Mansfield Park*, *Emma*, *Northanger Abbey* and *Persuasion*.

11) I know: that no-one can do everything.

12) Please reply: as soon as possible.

Semi-colons

A semi-colon can be used to join two sentences closely related in meaning. Consider these two short sentences:

She was very tired. She had worked late the night before.

There is a strong connection in meaning between these two sentences. Using a semi-colon instead of a full stop pinpoints the cause-and-effect connection.

She was very tired; she had worked late the night before.

Remember, however, that only complete sentences can be combined in this way and they must be related in meaning.

Semi-colons can replace commas in separating items in a list. If the items in a list are lengthy ones, already requiring commas for other reasons, the use of commas to separate one from another can be very confusing.

Pick your way through this sentence!

Each girl should bring these items with her: sturdy, well-fitting, watertight shoes, light, warm, loose clothing, a comfortable, lightweight rucksack, and essential items of backpacking equipment.

Use semi-colons to separate these items and the route is clearly signposted.

Each girl should bring these items with her: sturdy, well-fitting, water-tight shoes; light, warm, loose clothing; a comfortable, light-weight rucksack; and essential items of backpacking equipment.

Exercise 74

Use semi-colons instead of commas to separate the items in these lists.

1) There is much in the painting I could criticise: the composition is jumbled, with no focal point, the perspective is wrong, the brushwork is messy and unpleasing, and the subject has not been carefully and accurately observed.

2) I would make the following recommendations: the exterior of the house needs to be repointed, all external paintwork needs to be painted, the roof needs to be reslated as a matter of some urgency, the chimney stack should be made safe, the interior of the house needs to be redecorated throughout, and all internal woodwork should be treated as there is widespread evidence of woodworm activity.

3) She planned to plant the garden with all her favourite plants and shrubs: cream and golden honeysuckle with its beautiful fragrance, deep red antirrhinums with dark green slender leaves, an abundance of rose bushes, especially the old varieties with fragrant blooms, red, white and pink geraniums, she had to have those, and lastly marigolds, sturdy, shaggy, cheerful and golden, opening with the sun and closing regretfully in its absence.

4) My greatest regrets are these: that I did not know my parents, that I wasted so many years when I might have learnt much, that I did not take many of the opportunities that were offered to me to advance my career, and that I now dwell on the past to a disproportionate extent!

Exercise 75

In five of these sentences, the semi-colon has been used inappropriately. Identify the errors and correct them.

1) Alice was conscientious and able; she deserved to pass the examination.
2) The rabbit had been sadly neglected; it was in a wretched state.
3) Thinking that there was an intruder; Shaun grabbed a stick and rushed indoors.
4) Mrs Croal unpacked her shopping slowly; only to hear Karen at the door.
5) John opened the drawer; it was empty.

6) I will mark this set of books; Mrs Sims will be coming to supper tomorrow.

7) In fact; we shall all be there.

8) The wedding invitations have all been sent out; two hundred guests are expected.

9) I left immediately; I knew what had to be done.

10) I shall have to pay the bill; although I have no money to spare at the moment.

Chapter Seven

HYPHENS, DASHES, BRACKETS, OBLIQUES

Hyphens

There are six different circumstances in which you should use the hyphen. All of them involve joining.

A hyphen can indicate that a word continues on the next line.

This is a very familiar use of the hyphen, but it is surprising how many students use a hyphen at an inappropriate point in a word. You *don't* squeeze as much of the word in as you can, add a hyphen, and then carry on when you reach the next line. You should break the word at the end of a syllable.

√ **Mr Roberts said that the practice had been dis-
continued.**
√ **Mr Roberts said that the practice had been discon-
tinued.**
✗ **Mr Roberts said that the practice had been discontin-
ued.**

(Splitting a word before the last syllable, as in this last example, should be avoided.)

● The words must be divided at the end of a syllable to enable the reader to make sense of that part of the word and add quickly to it the remainder when it comes. Let pronunciation be your guide and choose a convenient break which does not distort the pronunciation of either part.

✗ **Mr Roberts said that the practice had been disco-
ntinued.**

Note how confusing the mid-syllable division makes the above sentence. The reader makes the best sense he or she can of *disco* and is entirely unable to make sense of *ntinued* without going back to the beginning of the word and putting it together again.

- The hyphen must appear with the first part of the word if it is to indicate effectively that there is more to come. It is a courtesy to the reader which should not be overlooked or delayed. (You don't need a hyphen on the next line as well.)

- It is probably best not to divide words at all if you can avoid it. It is a clumsy device at best and makes words look unfamiliar even when they are divided at a sensible point. If there's not room for the whole word at the end of a line, it's best to move on to the next.

- For obvious reasons, a one-syllabled word should not be divided, although some students regularly attempt it (**fin-d**, **an-d**, etc!!).

- Proper nouns should not be hyphenated.

  Avoid: **Pennsyl-vania, Ire-land**

Computer typesetting in newspaper offices often results in words being broken at inappropriate places at the ends of lines.

Exercise 76

In pairs, discuss the computer-set divisions of words in this short article. Which divisions seem to you to be sensible and which do you dislike and why?

1,400 city smokers died last year

EXETER has the second lowest figures for smoking-related deaths in the country.

But last year 1,400 people still died in the area because of their addiction to the evil weed.

And local Community Physician, Dr Dilwyn Morgan, says the current figures cannot be a cause for complacency.

In the second of a series of papers on preventing ill-health, he points out that smokers still risk death from lung cancer and diseases of the heart and blood vessels.

'In terms of absolute numbers coronary heart disease is the major killer among smoking-related diseases,' he says. 'Research has shown that the rewards for stopping smoking are immediate and substantial.'

His paper will be presented to the health authority tomorrow.

A survey on this age group showed that one in seven 11-year-olds had experimented with cigarettes; 18 per cent of 15-year-old boys and 27 per cent of the same-age girls smoked every week.

Dr Morgan also highlights other problems connected with smoking:

● Recent increases in the numbers of women dying of lung cancer.

● Absence from work because of recurrent chest infections.

● Smoking mothers double the risk of having a small baby.

● The aggravation of asthma in sufferers exposed to other people's smoke.

He commends the health authority for recognising that cigarette smoking is a serious public health hazard.

Express and Echo, 5 March 1990

A hyphen is used to make one word out of two or more words. Many nouns which we now write as one word were once written as two words. Many words which we now write as two words will one day be written as one word. There is an intermediate stage when the word is hyphenated. There is no firm demarcation line between one form and the next, and, for a generation or so two forms are likely to be correct. (If you are in doubt which form to use, your eye will probably help. Try writing the words separately, then hyphenate them, and then join them. Possibly one form will look right immediately.)

● Remember how helpful a good dictionary can be once you have learnt the symbols.

Under the heading 'watch' in the *Concise Oxford Dictionary,* for example, you will find:

~oil (This means you should write as two separate words: i.e. watch oil.)

~ -glass (This means you should hyphenate: i.e. watch-glass)

~'word (This means you should write as one word: i.e. watchword.)

Sometimes the instruction to write as one word or two words is not always so clear. For instance, under 'water' in the same dictionary we have:

~ bus (two words: i.e. water bus)
~side (one word: i.e. waterside)

In this entry, the gap between the symbol and the following word is the only clue.

Note:
Sometimes there is a difference in meaning between two forms and for that reason they will both exist in their own right. As we grow older, we may all come to use a walking-stick, and there is nothing unusual in that. However, you could make your fortune, at any age, from a 'walking stick'.

● Hyphens are also used to combine two or more words into a single adjective. Indeed hyphens can be vital to meaning. The compliment that you were 'a **hard-working** person' might fail to please if the hyphen were omitted. There is a substantial difference in meaning between 'a little used path' and 'a **little-used** path'.

Such compound adjectives need particular care. They can be made out of quite lengthy groups of words.

She had a **devil-may-care** lift to her chin.
James had an **I'm-better-than-you-whatever-you-may-think** expression in his eyes.
We are studying the **nineteenth-century** novelists.

Exercise 77

Read this short article from *The Independent* and in pairs discuss which words have been hyphenated to form compound adjectives and which have been hyphenated for other reasons.

Question of degree

ARE THE Scottish universities weakening in their defence of the four-year degree as the prospect of student loans draws nearer? Perish the thought.

The eight have, however, issued a statement reaffirming the value they attach to the three-year General or Ordinary degree available to undergraduates in Scotland.

The principals now wish to see this kind of broad-based degree given more prominence in its own right, rather than being seen as a truncated Honours degree. The curriculum is distinct from the early years of an Honours course, they say, adding that the General degree had proved of particular interest to mature students or those who intended to pursue further vocational studies.

With departments in Scottish universities preparing fall-back positions in case the three-year Honours degree seeps across the border, could this be an ingenious device to hold the line?

The Independent, 5 April 1990

Exercise 78

Use hyphens where necessary.

1) Lydia had a catch me if you can look in her eyes.

2) The scheme was well intentioned but ill conceived.

3) The poor child has been over protected all his life.

4) The wide eyed wonder and overwhelming amazement of the tiny boy on Christmas Day were very touching.

5) You should forward the doctor's signing off certificate as soon as you receive it.

6) The local candidate won in a three cornered fight.

7) The bereaved mother was naturally low spirited and depressed for months after the accident.

8) I can't find the nail scissors anywhere.

9) We decided to give Timothy a silver napkin ring for a christening present.

10) His couldn't care less attitude was infuriating to his parents and teachers alike.

Hyphens should be used with certain combinations of numbers. In the numbers between 20 and 100, hyphens should be used for all combinations of tens and units.

twenty-one	**thirty-four**	**eighty-nine**
twenty-first	**thirty-fourth**	**eighty-ninth**

Exercise 79

Write as words correctly punctuated. (This is also a useful spelling exercise!)

1.	99	99th	6.	27	27th
2.	88	88th	7.	62	62nd
3.	41	41st	8.	44	44th
4.	55	55th	9.	37	37th
5.	73	73rd	10.	96	96th

Three further uses of the hyphen.

● Hyphens can be used to suggest a range of dates and figures.

> **He fought in the 1914-18 war.**
> **Aunt Sophie wants to buy a bungalow in the £100,000-£120,000 price range.**

● Hyphens can be used to express routes.

> **The London-Exeter motorway is now completed.**
> **The Calais-Dover crossing is very cheap.**

- Hyphens can suggest hesitation or stammering in dialogue.

  I c-c-can't remember your n-name.

Exercise 80

Add hyphens where they are needed.

1) My uncle was killed in the 1939 45 war.
2) The Salisbury Portsmouth service is much improved.
3) It is m m more than m m my life is w w worth.
4) The Paris Melbourne race is cancelled.
5) The Exmouth Starcross ferry may be saved.
6) The Edinburgh London link up is a fruitful one.
7) The only car he can afford is in the £50 £75 price range.
8) Those who scored 80 100 per cent are excused from homework.
9) What a d d dreadful experience!
10) The London Manchester express has been derailed.

Dashes

Dashes look like long hyphens but they don't join. In fact, they separate by introducing pauses and hesitations.

There are four functions of the dash.

Four functions

- A dash can indicate a dramatic pause.

  Cedric Earle was lying at the foot of the stairs – dead.

- A dash can indicate hesitation.

  'I mean – I can't explain – forgive me – you must know how much – –.'

- A pair of dashes can be used like brackets.

  I bought some material – that was my first mistake – and settled down to an attempt at dressmaking.

- A dash can introduce an afterthought.

  We'll be leaving for Africa in July – whether we've sold our house or not.

These last two uses are often more appropriate in an informal letter. In formal writing, it is probably best to construct sentences more carefully. Dashes reflect the asides and interpolations of our conversation; our written style can be crafted with more care.

Note: Interpolated questions and exclamations do not require capital letters.

I bought some material – it was a big mistake! – and began to sew.
I bought some material – was it a big mistake? – and began to sew.

Exercise 81

Introduce a dash into each of the sentences below to add a dramatic pause.

1) The drawer was empty.

2) His jealousy knew no bounds and was quite murderous.

3) I looked at his long, pale face, with its cold eyes, and at his receding chin, and he reminded me very suddenly and very vividly of a fish.

4) I shall never marry.

5) What more need I say than that I give you my word?

6) In crawled a very shamefaced, very wet and very bedraggled small cat.

7) You are, sir, quite simply a liar.

8) One thing and one thing only has caused his downfall drink.

9) The answer to that question, madam, is never.

10) 'The reason for my long life,' quavered the centenarian, 'is undoubtedly my love of women.'

Exercise 82

Use nine dashes in the following hesitant speech.

'Mildred, if we are frank you must realise that is to say the fact is let me start again and say you've been very kind we don't deny we don't want that is nobody wants to hurt you.'

Exercise 83

Use dashes to mark off interpolations or introduce after-thoughts in the sentences below.

1) Your opinion however sincerely held could cause great offence.

2) The Managing Director to my horror he's a J.P. is an alcoholic.

3) She won the cup again this year would you believe it?

4) The owner believe it or not once worked for Harrods.

5) The Scotsman a keen golfer too antagonised all who came near him.

6) Do you know I waited it must have been for at least twenty minutes and no-one would serve me.

7) Write him a letter common courtesy will demand an apology and you will feel better about it.

8) Give him every chance he's a busy man to make amends.

9) The same thing happened to me I know it's hurtful.

10) There's no need to be anxious rather the reverse about what the outcome will be.

Exercise 84

Read the article from *The Independent* and in pairs answer these questions on dashes and hyphens used in the article.

CFC substitutes 'cause warming'

Substitutes for chlorofluorocarbons – the industrial gases attacking the earth's protective ozone layer – are powerful greenhouse gases which are likely to play a part in global warming unless their use is restricted.

The world's leading chemical companies are spending millions of pounds developing alternatives to CFCs which do much less or no harm to the ozone layer.

But three articles in the latest issue of the science journal *Nature* suggest that if these chemicals take over much of the old CFC market, and their production then continues to rise gradually, they will become important greenhouse gases in the next century, helping to alter climate and raise temperatures.

CFCs, which are used in refrigerators and as solvents and foam blowers, are being phased out under the Montreal Protocol. Their use as aerosol propellants has almost ended in many countries because of pressure from environmentalists and consumers.

The protocol calls for a 50 per cent cut in production by the end of the century, but it is now recognised that this will not save the ozone layer. Many countries, including Britain, are calling for a total phase-out by 2000.

The articles in *Nature* look at the impact of two types of CFC substitute, hydrochlorofluorocarbons (HCFCs) and hydrofluorocarbons (HFCs). HCFCs are in widespread use and being marketed as substitutes, even though they attack the ozone layer - albeit with less than one tenth the strength of CFCs, according to the research published yesterday. HCFCs will have to be phased out within the next 30 years.

Concern is focusing on HFCs, the next generation of substitutes soon to go into production which are seen as long-term CFC replacements. They do no harm to the ozone layer because they contain no chlorine, but like CFCs and HCFCs they are strong greenhouse gases.

According to scientists from Du Pont, the American chemicals giant, and a US research company, the global warming effect of HFC 134a is about a quarter that of CFC 11. HFC 134a is the front running substitute for CFCs in refrigeration.

Dr Keith Shine, of Reading University's Meterology Department, says the research shows that 'ozone friendliness' does not imply 'greenhouse friendliness'. If the HCFCs and HFCs took over slightly less than half the market for CFCs, then grew by 2.5 per cent a year, they would be responsible for about a tenth of global warming in the next century.

By Nicholas Schoon

The Independent, 5 April 1990

1) What is the function of the pair of dashes in the first paragraph?

2) Why is the hyphen used in the last paragraph?

3) Explain the function of the hyphen in *phase-out* (end of paragraph five).

4) Why is the dash used in paragraph six?

5) Find an example of a compound adjective in the article.

Brackets

Aside and interpolations

We have already seen that a pair of commas or a pair of dashes can be used to mark off additional or interpolated material. Brackets also can be used for this purpose. Notice in the following examples how the interpolated information is increasingly isolated from the main body of the sentence. Brackets are the most powerful of the three punctuation marks used in these examples and they will sometimes be too powerful for your purpose.

> **My cousin, a dancer with the Royal Ballet Company, hopes very much to attend his 18th birthday party.**

> **My cousin – a dancer with the Royal Ballet Company – hopes very much to attend his 18th birthday party.**

> **My cousin (a dancer with the Royal Ballet Company) hopes very much to attend his 18th birthday party.**

- Square brackets are very convenient if you wish to add a comment of your own during the course of a quotation:

> Tribes of emerald-green grasshoppers leaped over his [**Clym's**] feet, falling awkwardly on their backs, heads or hips, like unskilful acrobats . . .
>
> Thomas Hardy, *The Return of the Native*

Exercise 85

Enclose asides and interpolations within brackets.

1) Tickets £1 each are available from Mrs Barlow.

2) Please contact the Hon. Secretary Mrs McFadden if you are able to help.

3) Which days in your school-life some 13 000 hours over the eleven years have been most memorable?

4) I know Mr Ley well he's got a heart of gold and I know he's to be trusted.

5) I approached the Severn Bridge I mistrust all bridges with some trepidation.

6) His funeral a poignant ceremony was attended by hundreds of admirers and friends.

7) Today what a treat for you all! we shall have dictation.

8) The last chapter the best written concludes his life in Wales.

9) We shall have sausages, mashed potato such an innocent form of the vegetable and baked beans.

10) Tickets members only will be on sale next month.

Exercise 86

Use five pairs of brackets where appropriate in the passage below.

If your child is really talented, then full-time training it is an expensive business is essential. It takes years to develop the muscular control of a dancer much damage can be done by the wrong approach and the very best professional help should be sought. So many bad habits particularly postural ones can be developed if the child is not closely supervised by an expert. A dancer's future can be ruined by a careless teacher. Three requirements must be met by aspiring dancers: they must have the right physique this is more than just being slim!; they must have the right personality and stage presence; and they must have as you would expect natural grace of movement.

Exercise 87

Read this extract from an article printed in *The Sunday Times* and answer the questions on hyphens, dashes and brackets which follow.

Battle of the bimbos

Feminism and greater awareness of role stereotypes have failed to kill off the fashion doll. But child's play has become big business, and Barbie and Sindy are heading for a showdown in court as two American corporations fight for supremacy in the £30m-a-year UK market.
Hugh Thompson *reports*

BARBIE, the American fashion doll – glamorous and silver-clad – is out on the town celebrating her pink jubilee (30 years and 500m sales) with her long-standing boyfriend Ken.

Suddenly she spies someone just as alluring. Why, it is 25-year-old Britisher Sindy with her equally glamorous long-standing boyfriend Paul. But is she wearing a similar frock? Has she done her hair the same way? Barbie cannot be sure. She cannot believe that her old friend would behave in such a jealous, competitive way and try to spoil the triumph of her jubilee.

Barbie refuses to speak to this remodelled Sindy. She rushes home and tells her daddy and mummy at the world's biggest toy company, Mattel, that Sindy's new look is simply a copy of the style she, Barbie, has made famous across the world.

So in May, Mattel took legal advice. In Belgium, an injunction has stopped all sales of the new-look Sindy. But Britain will have to wait until next year to find out the result of this tiff between two of the best-selling dolls in toyland history.

It is no laughing matter. Neither Mattel nor Hasbro, which owns Sindy, is prepared to go on the record. In fact, Hasbro is so defensive about the injunction that all it will say comes from its internal legal adviser, Michael McCooe. 'We have no comment to make on this story. You publish anything with regard to this story at your own risk.'

Even Britain's most famous toy shop, Hamleys, is nervous as the two American corporations tussle for domination of the world's doll counter. 'We stock both products. We don't want to sour our relations with either side, so I'm afraid it's no comment,' the store said.

For years Sindy was number one in the UK, while Barbie was the world's best-selling fashion doll. British girls preferred Sindy because she was less over-the-top than her American cousin.

However, in the 1980s Barbie, with the help of television advertising, overtook Sindy on her home patch. Soaps such as Dallas and Dynasty made the more ostentatious Barbie preferable to her girl-next-door rival.

In 1987 Sindy was sold by her founders, Pedigree, to the American toy giant Hasbro, which relaunched her – and now she does look more like the world's number one. Sindy's packaging has been changed to pink, which traditionally has been Barbie's colour.

Although to young girls they may only be dolls, to the two companies they are big business. Fashion dolls in the UK are a £30m-a-year market, with Barbie taking 55% and Sindy 35%.

With the number of four- to nine-year-old girls in Britain set to grow from 2m to 2.4m by 2000, it is an expanding market. In a recent survey, the researchers Projection 2000 said: 'No amount of feminist or anti-sexist propaganda has killed off even the most blatantly role-stereotyped dolls.'

© *The Sunday Times*, 23 July 1990

1) Why has a pair of dashes been used in the first sentence? Consider using a pair of commas, and a pair of brackets instead. Which do you prefer and why?

2) Do you approve of the pair of brackets used later in this first sentence? What other punctuation marks could be substituted? Which do you think best suits the purpose here?

3) Explain clearly why 'long-standing' in the second paragraph is hyphenated.

4) There are three cases in this article where words at the end of a line are hyphenated because they form part of a compound adjective continued on the next line. Find them.

5) Why has the dash been used in paragraph nine? What other punctuation marks could be substituted with what different effects?

Obliques

The oblique (short for 'oblique stroke') is a useful punctuation mark in certain very restricted instances. It is used when space is limited, such as in questions on official forms and so on. It is only rarely correct to use obliques in essays and other pieces of extended writing.

● Obliques can neatly separate alternative items or various forms.

> **The god Neptune/Poseidon emerged from the sea.**
> (The god has a Latin name and a Greek name)
> **Use 100g cocoa/drinking chocolate.**
> **Please list interests/hobbies/recreations.**

As you will see in the above examples, the oblique can be a useful, concise device in notes, or on official forms, or in recipes, etc. It is not to be recommended for use in more formal writing, except as used in the first example.

● Obliques are used to separate items in a list
(e.g. lists of destinations or ports of call).

> **The train travels via Exmouth/Topsham/Polsloe Bridge/ St James's Halt/Exeter Central/Exeter St David's.**

● Obliques can be used with certain combinations of figures.

> **Date of birth: 9/8/37**

(This is a useful way of recording dates where space is limited, such as on a form.)

> **My telephone number is 03982/31085.**

(Here the oblique divides the dialling code from the number itself. Alternatively, the dialling code could be bracketed or a hyphen could be used.)

- Obliques are traditionally used in certain abbreviations.

c/o Mrs Abrahams (care of)
T/A Owls' Retreat Tutorial Services (trading as)
a/c (account)

Exercise 88

Use 10 obliques where appropriate on this form.

Name (Mr Mrs Miss Ms):

Date of birth:

Address:

Telephone number (day evening):

Qualifications (academic professional):

Previous posts held (indicate whether full part-time):

Present post:

Other relevant experience training:

Hobbies interests recreational activities:

Names and addresses of two referees:

(Write NA where a question is not applicable.)

ANSWERS

Exercise 1
1) . . . hungry.
3) . . . oven.
6) . . . morning.
10) . . . help.   . . . urgently.

Exercise 2
. . . morning.   . . . minutes.   . . . dress.
. . . meal.   . . . back.

Exercise 3
1) My grandfather is very old. He is still very active.
2) I'll arrange for you to be transferred to Hong Kong. You really dislike this area.
3) There has just been a news flash. There's been a terrible accident in the English Channel.
4) Cherrill thoroughly enjoyed the weekend. She spent it at Pontins.
5) The abolition of the poll tax has been rumoured. The rumour isn't true.

Exercise 4
By 9.30a.m. Wayne was already flagging. Tired and listless, he blinked a lot and often rubbed his hand over his face. He struggled on without either interest or enthusiasm.

By early afternoon the sun was shining brightly through the classroom windows. Wayne sat hunched forward over his desk supporting his head in his arms as he struggled to keep himself awake. By 3p.m., head cradled in his arms, he was asleep.

At 14, Wayne is one of thousands of youngsters up and down the country who spend their days in school teetering on the edge of exhaustion. Late nights, 24-hour television, satellite TV, the video revolution may all play a part but the most tired pupils in schools are, surprisingly, not those whose leisure pursuits keep them awake but rather those with part-time jobs which leave them tired and unable to concentrate.

At 14 Wayne, with parental knowledge, begins work at 4a.m. During the winter, if there are difficulties with snow he may start work even earlier. He is late for school most mornings after delivering milk for four or five hours and earning £3.50.

While there are nowhere near as many children 'on the milk' as there are 'on the papers' there are enough to give cause for concern. It is illegal for children to deliver milk at the time it is delivered but a 'blind eye' is frequently turned on such breaches.

The milk float in question is not the familiar slow battery-powered vehicle. This one is a flatbed, diesel truck and the round is big, around 300 gallons or 100 crates. The boys hang on, rain, hail or shine, to the bar at the rear of the vehicle and hop off nimbly with a full bottle carrier when the truck slows.

Brian Bell, *The Times Educational Supplement*, 4 August 1989

Exercise 5

(Suggested answers)

1) Jennifer is good at mathematics but Robert prefers history.
2) After opening the door of the deserted cottage, we felt frightened.
3) I felt concerned that something was wrong when the cat scratched her ear frantically.
4) He is shy and hard to get to know and few people know him well but he wants to be friendly and it is worth persevering.
5) Emily Bronte (pen name Ellis Bell) who wrote *Wuthering Heights* had two sisters who also wrote novels and used pen-names.

Exercise 6

(Suggested answers)

1) 'Would you like to appear in "Neighbours"?' he asked.
2) 'Why are you three hours late?' she demanded.
3) 'What is your name and address?' they asked.
4) 'Do you mean what you are saying?' he asked.
5) 'What are you going to give me for Christmas?' I asked.

Exercise 7

(Suggested answers)

1) The speaker asked the audience if he could be heard at the back.
2) His mother asked Matthew whether he had tidied his room yet.
3) Dr Jones looked over his glasses at his new patient and asked whether he was allergic to penicillin.
4) My neighbour wanted to know if I would give him a hand demolishing his garage on Sunday.
5) Mike proposed to Kate in a whisper.

Exercise 8

2) 'Have you got a large spanner I can borrow?'
4) 'Can I interest you in our special offer?'
5) 'What is the time?'
8) 'Are you going to wear that hat?'
10) 'Where are you going on holiday?'
11) 'Do you know the answer or are you bluffing?'
14) 'Are you certain?'
16) 'Why did she leave so suddenly?'
18) 'Why did you behave as you did?'
19) 'Was it snowing when you left Newcastle?'

Exercise 9

1) .	3) ?	5) ?	7) .	9) .
2) ?	4) ?	6) .	8) ?	10) ?

Exercise 11

1) .	5) ?	9) !	13) !	17) !
2) !	6) .	10) !	14) .	18) .
3) ?	7) .	11) .	15) !	19) ?
4) !	8) !	12) ?	16) !	20) .

Exercise 12

Jem	Who did one thing to help Tom Robinson?
Miss Maudie	His friends, for one thing, and people like us. We exist, too. People like Judge Taylor. People like Heck Tate. Start using your head, Jem. Did it ever strike you that Judge Taylor naming Atticus to defend Tom was no accident? That Judge Taylor might have had his reasons?
Scout	S'right, Jem. Usually the court appoints some new lawyer – one who is just startin'.
Miss Maudie	You're beginning to realise a little more to it than you thought. (Pressing). Whether Maycomb knows it or not, we're paying your father the highest tribute we can pay a man. We trust him to do it right.
Scout	Then why did he get beat?
Miss Maudie	(snorting): Miss Stephanie talks nonsense! Maybe he didn't get an acquittal but he got something. I was sitting right in court waiting, and as I waited, I thought – Atticus Finch won't win, he can't win, but he's the only man in these parts who can keep a jury out so long in a case like this. And I thought to myself, take note of this time and this place. It's 1935 and it's Maycomb, Alabama, and we're making a step – it's just a baby-step, but it's a step.

Exercise 13

1) Names and proper nouns
2) At beginning of a sentence
3) For pronoun I
4) First word and 'Brownie' in title
5) At beginning of direct speech
6) Eye-catching emphasis at beginning of article.

Exercise 14

In . . . country. Springs . . . nails.
Although . . . village. For . . . die. There . . . all.

Exercise 15

a) Paragraph 1 . . . myself. . . . anon.
 . . . us. . . . shoulders.
 Paragraph 2 . . . Walpole. (Whole paragraph is one sentence.)
 Paragraph 3 . . . robin.
 Paragraph 4 . . . bell? . . . pull.
 . . . architecture? . . . bullfinch.
 . . . and so on.
b) 11 times

Exercise 16

1) Thursday
2) Industrial Revolution
3) Portsmouth   Channel Islands
4) England   Queen Elizabeth
5) Mrs. Brown   Harriet
6) Spanish.
7) Owen   Cader Idris
8) Ombudsman   Prime Minister
9) Wednesday   March
10) Council   Preservation   Rural England

Exercise 17

1) God
3) Bible
4) Father, God, Son, God, Holy Spirit, Persons, Holy Trinity
5) Christianity, Judaism, Buddhism, Islam

Exercise 18

1) *A Village by the Sea*
2) *An Inspector Calls*
3) *Daily Telegraph*
4) *The Rise and Fall of the Smoking Habit*
5) *The Archers*
6) *Mathematics for the General Student*
7) *Jaws*

Exercise 19

Never . . .
Love . . .
For . . .
Silently . . .

I . . . I . . .
I . . .
Trembling . . .
Ah, . . .

Soon . . .
A . . .
Silently . . .
He . . .

Exercise 20

'Must I go . . . ?'
'You must . . .'
He pleaded, 'All . . .'
'Put me down,' he sobbed. 'Put . . .'

Exercise 21

Rose Cottage,
6 The Green,
Friary Park,
Cheshire, SK8 3EY

Monday, 20th August

Dear John,

We all enjoyed reading your letter. What a marvellous holiday in the United States you must have had! We all envy you horribly.

Is there any chance that we may see something of you at Easter? Do let us know if you can manage to spend a few days at least with us.

Fiona got good grades in her 'A' levels, I am glad to say, and she's now sure of her place at Queen Mary College (that's London University). Her geography result was better than we expected.

We're off on holiday next Saturday for three weeks on the Isle of Wight. We had to book our passage on the car ferry way back in March!

With every best wish,
Alison

Exercise 24

1) I've . . . it's . . .
2) He's . . . he'll . . .
3) They've . . . they're . . . o'clock.
4) 'Ang . . . 'at . . . 'ook . . . 'all. (Hang, hat, hook, hall)
5) We'll . . . '98.
6) It's . . . you've . . .
7) . . . japonica'd (i.e. covered in japonica)
8) . . . where'er . . . pass'd . . .
9) All's
10) You're

Exercise 25

1) p's   q's
2) 3R's
3) N.C.O.'s
4) 1960's
5) b's   d's
6) ◇'s   △'s
7) JCB's
8) under-12's
9) 7's
10) Q's
11) y's   j's

Exercise 26

1) . . . doesn't . . . he's
2) Don't
3) It's . . .
4) Who's . . .
5) I'm . . . it's . . .
6) . . . o'clock . . . everyone's . . .
7) They're . . . I'm . . . they'll . . . A's
8) He'll . . .
9) We're . . .
10) . . . shouldn't . . .
11) It's . . . they've . . .
12) . . . won't . . . you've . . .

Exercise 27

1) It's	3) its	5) it's	7) its	9) It's
2) it's	4) It's	6) it's	8) Its	10) It's

Exercise 28

1) It's	3) its	5) It's	7) It's	9) its
2) its	4) its	6) its	8) its	10) It's

Exercise 29

1) Who's	3) Whose	5) who's	7) Whose	9) whose
2) whose	4) whose	6) Who's	8) who's	10) Who's

Exercise 30

1) They're	3) they're	5) There	7) they're	9) there
2) their	4) They're	6) there	8) There	10) their

123

Exercise 31

1) You're	3) your	5) your	7) Your	9) Your
2) you're	4) Your	6) You're	8) you're	10) You're

Exercise 32

c is correct

Exercise 33

a) Posture, ... movements, ... relax, ... smiles,
b) ... gap, ... stalled, ... moment,
c) ... scene, background, (optional) ... situation, ... it, (optional)

Exercise 34

a) ... delays, ... children, ... meetings, ... appointment, ... boss,
b) ... fear, joy, aggression, (optional) ... dominating, aggressive, (optional)

Exercise 35

1) ..., I regret to say, ...
2) As you will know,
3) ..., isn't it?
4) In fact, ...
5) To put the story in a nutshell, ...
6) ..., or rather I expect, ...
7) Please, ...
8) ..., don't they?
9) In conclusion, ...
10) ..., however, ...

Exercise 36

1) ..., Mr. Evans.
2) ..., my love.
3) ..., Upper 3, ...
4) Anna and Matthew, ...
5) Mrs. Thompson, ...
6) ..., sir, ...
7) Doctor, ...
8) ..., ladies
9) Ladies and gentlemen, ...
10) Karen, ...

Exercise 37

1) , Matt Streat,
2) , Edward Hallett,
3) , the Chancellor of the Exchequer,
4) , Blackie and Sooty
5) , Norman Sherry,
6) , Mary,
7) , Louis Cooper,
8) , her parents' golden wedding anniversary,
9) , a newly privatised company,
10) , your husband,

124

Exercise 38

1) ..., biting her fingernails anxiously.
2) Subdued at last, ...
3) ..., putting the matter entirely out of her mind,
4) Not believing in miracles any more, ...
5) Refusing help, ...
6) ..., placing it with the others in the china cupboard, ...
7) Exhausted by the long wait for the bus, ...
8) ..., watching their reactions very shrewdly.
9) Sipping her sherry, ...
10) ..., slipping quietly into the office, ...

Exercise 39

1) As he was tired, Shaun decided to go home early.
3) Shaun decided, as he was tired, to go home early.
5) Because he is not in the best of health, Mr White is retiring early.
6) If you accept our invitation to come for Christmas, we shall all be delighted.
8) When Matthew sat the entrance examination, he was very nervous at first.
9) Wherever you go, you will see the same thing.
10) Unless you complain officially about the noise, nothing will be done.
11) At last Mr Wilson agreed that, if the doctor insisted, he would take a holiday.
12) As her boyfriend was behaving so abominably, Lydia decided to give him up.
15) After she posted the letter, she started to cry.

Exercise 40

Commas are needed in the following sentences: 3, 5, 6, 9.

Exercise 41

1) ... again,'
2) ... wistfully, 'We've ...
3) ... presents,'
4) ... regret,' said the headmaster, 'having ...
5) ... said, 'Can ...
6) ... conversation,' said Miss Brewster, 'but ...
7) ... go out,' said Alan's mother, 'and ...

Exercise 42

... in three weeks' time, although ...

Exercise 43

... knew him, partly ...
... service, and mourned ...
... Devon, as he would have wished.

Exercise 45
Traditional layout

33 Willow Road,
Charlton Kings,
CHELTENHAM,
Gloucestershire

June 16th, 1991

The Editor,
The Times,
1 Pennington Street,
LONDON
E1 9XN

Dear Sir,

(Paragraphing as in printed version)

Yours faithfully,
Eric Chisholm
(ERIC CHISHOLM) (optional)

Fully-blocked layout

33 Willow Road
Charlton Kings
CHELTENHAM
Gloucestershire

16 June 1991

The Editor
The Times
1 Pennington Street
LONDON
E1 9XN

Dear Sir

Could I offer ....

....

After years of indecision ....

....

Yours faithfully

Eric Chisholm
(ERIC CHISHOLM) (optional)

Exercise 46

1) , an experienced cyclist,
2) to offer them,
4) , however,
5) James asked, 'What . . . tonight, Mum?'
6) boots, plimsolls, sandals, walking-shoes, flip-flops, (optional)
7) . . . emotion,
8) '. . . , everyone. Do sit down,' . . .
9) question,

Exercise 47

1) piano, guitar, descant recorder, treble recorder, (optional)
2) , ladies and gentlemen,
3) , Mrs Greenham,
4) . . . next week,'
5) Laughing uncontrollably,
6) . . . in stock,'
7) washing up,
8) , who is extremely house-proud,
9) Madam,
10) work,

Exercise 48

1) , a beautiful tabby,
2) Yes, . . . , Simon.
3) , which is open . . . Day,
4) Tuesday,
5) , moreover,
6) Italy, Greece, France, Spain, Norway, (optional).
7) , which is . . . comprehensive,
8) weight,
9) '. . . know,' he said, 'that . . .'
10) letters, . . . house, . . . bed, (optional).

Exercise 49

1) Have you met my mother-in-law, Mrs Allen?
2) What a frightful experience for you all!
3) 'Now we shall never know,' Mr Cobley said in conclusion, 'whether the treasure, a priceless collection of precious stones, was ever on board the *Santa Veronica*.'
4) Help!
5) The friend who has helped me most since I have been ill is my next-door neighbour, Brenda Carter.
6) Cauliflower, cabbage, brussels sprouts, (optional) and purple-sprouting broccoli should be planted now.

7) As they rounded the bend, they saw the horrifying sight before them.
8) Smiling nervously, William shook Mr Thorpe's hand.
9) Did you see all the instalments of *Brideshead Revisited*?
10) 'Sugar!' the old lady exclaimed.

Exercise 50

1) '. . . know,' said John Brown, 'that . . .'
2) , despite her earlier objections,
3) matches, . . . five, three (optional)
4) , a fledgeling,
5) childhood,
6) , in fact,
7) Mr Brown,
8) exhausting, expensive, time-consuming, (optional)
9) , whispering softly,
10) herself, accountant (optional)
11) clear, concise (optional)

Exercise 51

c) appearance, Alix would say, hard speculative gaze, cheeks, smudged, appearance, colour off, hair, dressing table, neck, combs, ears,

Exercise 52

1) The commas enclose an aside.
2) The comma introduces a phrase in apposition to 'psychoanalyst'.
3) False. The comma introduces a phrase in apposition to 'withdrawn state'.
4) The comma separates an item in a list.
5) Commas around the clause would dilute the meaning, and would make the reference to 'total security in early childhood' seem *incidental*, instead of being *vital* as a contrast to the shock of being sent to boarding school at so young an age.

Exercise 53

1) 'Have . . . vegetarian?' the . . .
2) 'You . . . haircut,' said . . .
3) 'How . . . fat!' Shaun's . . .
4) 'Kate . . . again,' whispered . . .
   or 'Kate . . . again!' whispered . . .
5) 'Ian . . . Friday,' Anna . . .

Exercise 54

1) The ... calmly, 'Stop ... now.'
2) Clair ... whispered, 'Would ... milk?'
3) Both ... together, 'No, ... fair!'
   or Both ... together, 'No, ... fair.'
4) The ... said, 'Here ... licence.'
5) Mr MacBean ... despairingly, 'How ... truth?'

Exercise 55

1) 'Does ... ticket,' Alison shouted, 'for ... Birmingham?'
2) 'If ... you,' snapped the irate chemistry teacher, 'then ... today.'
3) 'Before ... matinee,' announced Mrs King, 'we'll ... Garden.'
4) 'I've ... weeks,' pouted Claire, 'and ... ounce.'
5) 'Why ... us,' suggested Matthew, 'and ... home?'

Exercise 56

1) 'Thank ... help,' said Mrs Greenham. 'It ... appreciated.'
2) 'I ... us,' said Juliet quiety. 'I ... job.'
3) 'It's ... happened,' the police constable said. 'We ... further.'
4) 'We ... exercises,' Miss Jones said. 'In ... new.'
5) 'I'm ... now,' said John. 'It's ... today.'
6) 'The ... things,' announced their father. 'Now ... room.'
7) 'I'm ... now,' smiled Ann-Marie. 'I've ... morning.'
8) 'When ... while,' their mother said. 'I ... o'clock.'
9) 'We ... picture,' announced Anna Ford. 'Meanwhile ... music.'
10) 'Your ... yesterday,' said the woman. 'It ... relief.'

Exercise 57

'How ... Snowy?' asked Aunt Gladys.
'We ... ago,' answered her nephew. 'A friend ... love to have him.'
'Do ... attention?' asked his aunt.
'No ... pets,' he said. 'I ... garden.'
'Does ... vegetables?'
'I ... off!'
'He's ... thing,' smiled Aunt Gladys. 'Perhaps ... too.'

Exercise 58

The dog, who was sitting on the garden path, saw her first and got up with a welcoming bark. Mr Blake looked up from his weeding.
   'Sadie! Anything wrong?'
   'No.'

He came to the gate. 'You don't look your usual bouncy self.'

'It's just that I've got the sack and Mrs McConkey is dead. Mrs McConkey kept the shop near us.'

'I see.'

'I wanted someone to talk to. So I thought I'd come and see you.'

'Come in.'

They sat in the kitchen. Sadie rested her folded arms on the kitchen table.

'We always used to make fun of Mrs McConkey,' she sighed. 'We would shout names at her when we were small and then run like blazes before she could get hold of us. She never did because she was too fat. And now she's dead.'

'Aye, it's bad, Sadie, there's no denying it. Scarcely a day goes by without somebody getting killed, but when it's a person you know it's not so easy to take.'

'It's not easy at all,' said Sadie.

Exercise 59

1) now,'
2) answered my mother,'
3) can come,' smiled Mrs Thompson.
4) late?' asked Nicola.
5) said, 'All
6) home?' called
7) language,' boasted
8) immediately, 'Well,
9) 'Help!' cried
10) thought,' commented

Exercise 60

'There's been a mistake and I've come to explain,' said Ruth in Polish. 'This is Jan. It's all his fault. I want to speak for him.'

The interpreter translated.

'Who is the other child?' said Captain Greenwood.

'My sister Bronia,' said Ruth. 'She has nothing to do with this, but I had to bring her along as I've nowhere to leave her. We're on our way to Switzerland and are camping by the mill-stream.'

'I see. What's the boy's full name?' said Captain Greenwood.

'Only Jan – that's the only name of his we know,' said Ruth.

'Jan, have you any parents?' said Captain Greenwood.

'The grey cat and Jimpy, but they're dead, and Ruth's my mother now,' said Jan, sullenly.

Captain Greenwood could make nothing of this. Ruth did her best to explain a situation she did not fully understand herself.

'We take it then that you have no parents, but that this young lady, Ruth Balicki, aged eighteen, sister of Edek Balicki, is your guardian,' said Captain Greenwood.

Exercise 61

'What . . . weaknesses?' Miss Meloy asked.

'I know my spelling is pretty awful and I'm always making punctuation mistakes,' replied Geoffrey.

'You need plenty of practice then,' his teacher said. 'That can be arranged easily enough. Are you prepared to do extra homework?'

'I am very willing,' replied Geoffrey.

Exercise 62

1) 'I mustn't . . . flour,' muttered Aunt Elsie.
2) 'It . . . late,' said Mr Wilkens firmly, 'to . . . punctuate.'
3) 'Uncle Fred,' asked James quietly, 'do . . . shed?'
4) 'I . . . you'll . . . evening,' smiled their mother. 'We'll have roast chicken with two vegetables, followed by chocolate pudding and cream. Will that satisfy you?'
5) 'Excuse me. Have you lost your purse?'
   'No, I haven't but thank you for asking.'

Exercise 63

'Will you print my poems if I send them to you – the remaining ones in the sequence?'

'No. Who wants to read your poems?' Murad said at once, abruptly. 'I have enough poems for the issue already. As soon as I sent out the circular announcing it, contributions started pouring in. Poems, poems, poems. Everybody writes them, I tell you,' he complained, plucking at his hair in mock distress.

Exercise 64

1) 'Antony and Cleopatra' 'Romeo and Juliet'.
2) 'The Mill on the Floss'.
3) 'In Memoriam'.
4) —
5) 'The Sunday Times' 'The Observer'
6) 'Evening Express'
7) —
8) 'Dandy'
9) 'Panorama'
10) 'Anna Karenina'

Exercise 66

1) the pupils' questions
2) the audience's response
3) the crowd's roar
4) the frog's hop
5) the flowers' fragrance
6) the boy's enthusiasm
7) the women's bright dresses
8) the policemen's voices
9) the witnesses' evidence
10) the mouse's tail

Exercise 67
1) the butterflies' antennae
2) the cat's paw
3) the ladies' waiting room
4) the children's games
5) the car's headlights
6) the clock's hands
7) the footmen's wigs
8) the manager's decision
9) the ambassador's wife
10) the aldermen's wives

Exercise 68
1) bride's
2) moment's
3) ladies' and gentlemen's
4) Members'
5) —
6) children's
7) gentlemen's
8) princesses'
9) Morris's
10) Citizens'

Exercise 69
1) Harris's bride's
2) year's
3) Booklovers'
4) —
5) workmen's
6) Headmasters' Teachers'
7) Builders'
8) children's
9) day's
10) —

Exercise 70
heaven's sake (apostrophe misplaced)
Adamsons' party (apostrophe omitted)
life's leaders (apostrophe omitted)
Townswomen's Guild
    (apostrophe misplaced)
Birdwatchers' Circle
    (apostrophe omitted)

Exercise 71
Davy's . . .
government's . . .
deputies' . . .
New Year's . . .
umpire's . . .

Exercise 72
1) everything:
2) require:
3) boot:
4) her:
5) eyes:
6) letter:
7) brassicas:
8) stolen:
9) subjects:
10) shrines:

Exercise 73
1) Here are apples . . .
3) We visited Brussels . . .
7) She planned to clean . . .
11) I know that no-one . . .
12) Please reply as soon . . .

Exercise 74
1) . . . point; . . . wrong; . . . unpleasing;
2) . . . repointed; . . . painted; . . . urgency; . . . safe; . . . throughout;
3) . . . fragrance; . . . leaves; . . . blooms; . . . those;
4) . . . parents; . . . much; . . . career;

Exercise 75

3) Thinking that there was an intruder,
4) Mrs Croal unpacked her shopping slowly,
6) I will mark this set of books. Mrs. Sims will be coming to supper tomorrow.
7) In fact, we
10) I shall have to pay the bill although I have no money to spare at the moment.

Exercise 78

1) catch-me-if-you-can
2) well-intentioned   ill-conceived
3) over-protected
4) wide-eyed
5) signing-off
6) three-cornered
7) low-spirited
8) —
9) —
10) couldn't-care-less

Exercise 79

1) ninety-nine   ninety-ninth
2) eighty-eight   eighty-eighth
3) forty-one   forty-first
4) fifty-five   fifty-fifth
5) seventy-three   seventy-third
6) twenty-seven   twenty-seventh
7) sixty-two   sixty-second
8) forty-four   forty-fourth
9) thirty-seven   thirty-seventh
10) ninety-six   ninety-sixth

Exercise 80

1) 1939–45
2) Salisbury–Portsmouth
3) m-m-more   m-m-my   w-w-worth
4) Paris–Melbourne
5) Exmouth–Starcross
6) Edinburgh–London
7) £50–£75
8) 80–100 per cent
9) d-d-dreadful
10) London–Manchester

Exercise 81

(Suggested answers)
1) The drawer was – empty.
2) His jealousy knew no bounds and was quite – murderous.
3) I looked . . . and very vividly – of a fish.
4) I shall – never marry.
5) What . . . give you – my word.
6) In crawled . . . very bedraggled – small cat.
7) You are . . . simply – a liar.
8) One . . . downfall – drink.
9) The answer . . . is – never.
10) The . . . undoubtedly – my love of women.

Exercise 82

'Mildred, if we are frank – you must realise – that is to say – the fact is – let me start again and say – you've been very kind – we don't deny – we don't want – that is – nobody wants to hurt you.'

Exercise 83

1) – however sincerely held –
2) – to my horror he's a J.P. –
3) – would you believe it?
4) – believe it or not –
5) – a keen golfer too –
6) – it must have been for at least twenty minutes –
7) – common courtesy will demand an apology –
8) – he's a busy man –
9) – I know it's hurtful
10) – rather the reverse –

Exercise 84

1) separates phrase in apposition to 'chlorofluorocarbons'.
2) indicate word continues on next line.
3) compound noun.
4) introduces an aside or additional comment.
5) long-term (para 7)

Exercise 85

1) (£1 each)
2) (Mrs McFadden)
3) (some 13 000 hours over the eleven years)
4) (he's got a heart of gold)

5) (I mistrust all bridges)
6) (a poignant ceremony)
7) (what a treat for you all!)
8) (the best written)
9) (such an innocent form of the vegetable)
10) (members only)

Exercise 86
(it is an expensive business)
(much damage can be done by the wrong approach)
(particularly postural ones)
(this is more than just being slim!)
(as you would expect)

Exercise 88
Mr/Mrs/Miss/Ms
day/evening
academic/professional
full/part-time
experience/training
hobbies/interests/recreational activities
N/A